A QUIET STRENGTH

THE LIFE AND LEGACY OF
Jeannette M. Cathy

Trudy Cathy White

TRUDY CATHY WHITE

Forefront
BOOKS

A Quiet Strength
The Life and Legacy of Jeannette M. Cathy

Published by Forefront Books.

Cover Design by Bruce Gore, Gore Studio Inc.
Interior Design by Bill Kersey, KerseyGraphics

ISBN: 978-1-948677-35-6
ISBN: 978-1-948677-36-3 (eBook)

Table of Contents

INTRODUCTION

You Can

Author's Note: Even though my mother was an open and friendly person, she was surprisingly private. If you'd have met her, you'd have seen that she would much rather talk about you than about herself. That warmth and others-first mentality was part of her charm. However, it also made her reluctant to talk about herself very often. So when she did, people listened. One such occasion was a speech she delivered to a group of ladies at a Christian women's retreat in 2007. Here, I want to present the text of that presentation using my mother's own notes. I can think of no better opening for this memoir of her life than to let my mother introduce herself.

ow in the world did I come to this moment, being asked to speak to all of you today? At eighty-five years old, I'm honored and amazed at what the Lord would have me do. It has been an interesting journey all my life.

I first believed in God when I was very young, and that faith has always been my anchor. In faith, I found that I've been able to do far more than I ever imagined. Over the years, the Lord has taught me two powerful little words that have led me into more opportunities, joys, and challenges than I ever expected. These two words are always with me—even now as I stand here with you. Those two powerful words are *you can*.

I have a little book titled *You Can* that is a collection of essays, ideas, and thoughts about success in any endeavor by great thinkers like Henry David Thoreau, Napoleon Hill, Benjamin Franklin, Winston Churchill, and others going all the way back to William Shakespeare. These stories give me inspiration and strength. I have attempted many things in my life when I felt it was something God wanted me to do, and I discovered I *could* do them when I heard the Lord whisper, "You can."

Let's say these two great words out loud: YOU CAN. I think we can do anything we set our minds to as long as we keep telling ourselves *you can*. I know that's been true in my life.

I will share my life story because, well, I know it best. I was born on December 23, 1922, and raised in Atlanta, Georgia. My mother and father had a short life together. He left when I was just three months old. I lived with my mother and grandparents in the same house for many years, and I knew they all loved me. It was during this time that I first went to church and found out that I had a heavenly Father who loved me, too, and I believed in Him.

The Great Depression hit and Grandfather was out of work. Mother took in sewing and spent most of her time making costumes for little girls at dancing schools. A teacher at one of the schools offered to teach me tap dancing, acrobatics, and ballet. Mother loved to make costumes for my performances. I also learned to sing. At three years old, I sang at the Lowes Grand Theatre in Atlanta and was the youngest performer. Most of the time when I tried to curtsy—with one foot behind the other and with my short legs—I ended up sitting right down on the stage!

Our neighborhood had a few small theaters, and they had amateur nights on Fridays and Saturdays. People would perform—singing, dancing, and playing instruments. Then, all the performers were brought out and lined up and someone would hold their hand over each one as the audience clapped for their favorite. I was so small and must have entertained them so much that I won the five- or ten-dollar prizes almost every time I entered!

A contest for performers from all over Atlanta had many competing for an entire week. Each night, the audience voted on the best entertainer and that person was given a gold medal. I performed on Friday and won for that night. Then, all the winners from Monday to Friday were brought on stage and the audience selected *me* as winner for the whole week. At just six years old, I won a silver loving cup trophy and was crowned the best dancer in Atlanta!

My mother and I later moved to West End in Atlanta and attended West End Baptist Church where we were baptized together. One day while Mother was ironing, I talked with her about my singing both at churches and on the public stage every weekend. I told her I felt it wasn't right for me to "sing for the devil" on Fridays and Saturdays and then "sing for the Lord" on Sundays. She told me it was up to me to make that choice and whatever I decided would be all right with her. I knew she loved to make beautiful costumes for me, but my decision was made and that was the end of my dancing and singing in theaters.

At that time, I was often asked to sing solos in Sunday School assemblies and churches. When people would ask me to sing at their church, they would come pick me up and take me home. On one occasion, a young woman had me sing for her business club that met at a downtown church. Afterward, she gave me a little book that I still have to this day, and she signed it *Esther Cathy*. Esther was one of six children and her large family, the Cathys, lived just two houses down from us.

Later, Esther's sister Agnes (who married a young preacher studying at Mercer College) asked Mother if they could take me with them one summer to several small churches where her husband, Dock Edwards, served as pastor. I was the guest soloist for one week of revival services at each of his churches, and I was so short that I had to stand in a chair behind the podium to sing! The churches were so small and poor that they sometimes paid Dock with bags of sweet potatoes, watermelons, eggs, and even chickens. I remember watching them strap the chicken cages to the running boards on the side of his car just to get them home.

Each week when we returned home from one of the revivals, we had to stop by the Cathy's boarding house to drop off the produce for Mrs. Cathy, Agnes's mother. She used it to feed her residents. On one of those early visits to the Cathy home, I remember seeing two little boys running on the porch. I later found out the boys were Truett and his brother Ben, the youngest of the Cathy clan. Truett and I went to the same grammar school and junior high, but he was one year ahead of me, so I really didn't get to know him. He's since told me that he sometimes spoke to me back then, but I don't remember much about him in those days.

After graduating from an all-girl high school—that's right, *no boys*—I secured a job in the accounting department of the government and worked in Atlanta. A lady I worked with invited me to go to Ridgecrest Baptist Assembly in Asheville, North Carolina, one summer. We spent several summers there, using our vacation time from work. While at Ridgecrest that first summer, I felt that my heavenly Father wanted me to prepare for some kind of Christian service for Him. I mentioned this to my church's ladies' class (a very large group at West End Baptist Church), and they said they would pay my way to New Orleans Baptist Seminary.

No one at the government accounting office could believe I was willing to give up that job to go off to school. But I did go. I left my job, packed what I had, and boarded the *Nancy Hanks* train that ran from Atlanta to New Orleans. While at seminary, I enjoyed all my studies and the extra activities that were promoted in and around New Orleans, such as street missions and trips outside the city where we held small services—sometimes under a tree or wherever else we could meet. We had portable fold-up pianos that I sometimes played during our worship time.

I really enjoyed Bible study in the classroom, but when it came time to choose my classes for the next quarter of study, I found I wasn't eligible for many subjects because those classes required a college degree as a prerequisite. I was quite concerned about this and mentioned it in my letters and conversations to my friends at West End Baptist Church. The ladies must have felt it would be good for me to enter college after my first year at New Orleans, and I was delighted when I learned they wanted to financially support me in that. I chose Bessie Tift College in Forsyth, Georgia, an all-girl school that later merged with another college and became Mercer University. After graduating from Tift,

I returned to New Orleans Seminary and enjoyed taking classes that I wasn't able to before as a religious education student.

At times, I wondered if I was going to marry one of the preacher boys at New Orleans Seminary. I did date a few of them, but my heavenly Father had other plans for me. During my time there, another Cathy sister, Gladys, had my mother make a beautiful white satin dress for her daughter to wear in her piano recital. Gladys asked my mother about me and found out I was in New Orleans and would be coming home for the Easter holiday. Gladys thought it would be great if her brother Truett would come pick me up and take me over to her house for a spaghetti supper during Easter weekend.

Two years before—in 1946—Truett and his brother Ben had recently returned from their service in the Army and had bought a small lot, pooled their resources together, and built a small restaurant called the Dwarf Grill (which we later renamed Dwarf House) in Hapeville, Georgia, near the big Ford plant. Truett was completely committed to its success. He rented a room in a house next door to the restaurant and was on call twenty-four hours, day and night, in case he needed to run back to work or fill in for someone.

When I completed my studies at New Orleans Seminary, I returned home and that was when Truett and I began our courtship. That little grill played a big role in our dating. From the first week, the restaurant was always closed on Sundays, so that was definitely a date night which consisted of attending church and then going by the grill to check on things. Truett made sure the ice bin and coolers were working (so they wouldn't be surprised by spoiled meat on Monday morning), then we would sit at the counter to have a Coke and listen to the jukebox.

Once in a while, we would have a date night at the movie theater. However, Truett was always so tired after working such long hours, so when he relaxed and got still, he usually fell asleep. I would have to wake him up when the movie was over!

Somehow during this busy season, Truett and his older brother Horace made time to build a small, four-room house about two miles from the grill. Truett and I were married in September 1948 and moved into that little house on Sylvan Road to begin our life together.

Tragedy struck not long after we married when both of Truett's brothers were killed in an airplane crash. Without Ben to help with the restaurant, Truett suddenly carried the full responsibility of the business. As he brought the bills and money home, I helped by taking care of the checks and deposits. I knew the Bible taught that ten percent of all we have belongs to God, and I told Truett about how I had always kept a record of the money I had and how I'd always given a tithe to the church. We agreed this would be a key value in our marriage and business, no matter how much or how little money we had. Soon after, I started working at the grill as a cashier and waitress to help out.

I describe the next several years this way: There were two of us from 1948–1952. Then, in 1953, we had a boy. In 1954, another boy. In 1955, a girl. In 1956, we rested and focused on our family and business. Then, in 1957, we outgrew our small house with three children and moved into another small house on a 262-acre farm. Fifty years later, we still live in the same farm-house—although we've added a couple of rooms onto it. That's where we raised our three lively children. They loved to ride horses and trail bikes on the farm, and we now have our grandchildren coming down to entertain their friends and enjoy the open space.

All through the years, we were always active in church. When we were young, Truett and I were regular members of West End Baptist Church where I continued singing solos. I also taught

Sunday School, was in choir, and played the piano. Then we attended Jefferson Avenue Baptist Church in East Point, where I was the Vacation Bible School superintendent. Finally, when we moved to the farm, we attended Lovejoy Baptist Church, a small church where I played piano and where Truett and I both taught Sunday School classes.

Because we were in the restaurant business, we always had a chance to provide food for various groups. One memorable Easter morning, we were preparing an early breakfast for the church. I'll never forget it. I lit the gas oven in the stove. Then, somehow, when I opened the oven door, flames shot out, melting the nylon stockings right off my legs and singing my eyebrows! Although it wasn't funny at the moment, we later laughed. That's what I call putting yourself into your work!

When our children were young, Truett began focusing on how to cook chicken, which he wanted to add to the grill menu. It was at this time that he came up with the Chick-fil-A® sandwich and put it on the menu at the Dwarf House. Business was good and people enjoyed his unique sandwich concept, so he tried putting his Chick-fil-A sandwich in other restaurants. However, he was not satisfied with the way anyone else prepared it and he ended his deals with the other restaurants.

We later renamed the restaurant Chick-fil-A after Truett's signature sandwich, and he began focusing all his energy on growing Chick-fil-A as a business. We now have 1,365 locations across the country.[1] After opening office space in a nearby building and leaving himself room to expand, business grew and we built our headquarters on forty-five acres near the Atlanta airport. We

---

1   Direct Selling Association, "Direct Selling in the United States: 2017 Facts and Data," June 18, 2018, https://www.dsa.org/docs/default-source/research/dsa_2017_factsanddata_2018.pdf.

joined the National Restaurant Association and made trips to the headquarters in Chicago many times to the annual restaurant show. I have fond memories of Truett's secretary and I donning our white outfits with a tiny chef's hat and offering Chick-fil-A samples to the conference attendees.

I have supported Truett in all his endeavors 100 percent. I've also encouraged our children in all they do, and all three are talented, well-spoken, and gifted in many ways. Dan, our oldest, is now the president of Chick-fil-A; Donald "Bubba" is over our philanthropy endeavors and works with our family and marriage ministries; and Trudy works with our Impact 360 program, a year-long program between high school and college, and she is the director for WinShape Camps for Girls.

I'm often asked, "Did you ever think when you built the first grill that you'd eventually go nationwide?" I always give the same answer: no. No, we weren't focused on going nationwide; we were content just taking each day at a time and were glad to make it through the day. And we were just so thankful that the Lord had been so gracious to us to allow us to have an opportunity to share with people. It's our privilege to encourage people—especially young people. That's the one thing you can never get enough of: encouragement.

We've had so many opportunities over the years, and we've tried to be faithful whenever the Lord's given us something to do. I believe we can each do incredible things for Him when we say, in faith, *you can.*

—Jeannette McNeil Cathy, 2007

CHAPTER 1

A Child of the King

My mother never knew her father.

That's a fact of her life that I've known forever, but it's still sometimes hard for me to fully grasp. I was blessed with the most wonderful, godly, loving, supportive, hardworking, and patient father a girl could have hoped for. From my birth in 1955 until his death in 2014, he was either at my side, right next door, or just a phone call away. Even during the twenty-plus years I was separated from him by distance, I was never separated from him in spirit. He was my daddy, and I was his little girl. That has truly been one of the fundamental truths of my life.

My mother, however, didn't have that. Her father walked out on her and her mother when Mom was just three months old. Her parents had only been married a year. He never came back, never called, never wrote. From that point on, it was just my granny, a young single mother trying to get by on her own in the early

1920s, and my mother. Raising a child alone is hard enough *today*; my heart aches for the millions of strong single mothers moving mountains to support their children. But back in 1923, it must have felt impossible. How difficult must it have been for a young woman to provide for herself and a baby back then? What would the Great Depression have looked like in that situation? Somehow, though, Granny made it work. She was my mother's hero.

Granny was a gifted seamstress who managed to eke out a living doing what she loved, even with only an eighth-grade education. She was particularly fond of the arts—mainly theater and dancing—and had a special knack for theatrical costuming. Her first big job was creating the original curtains that hung in the historic Fox Theater in Atlanta. She did such a wonderful job that she was offered a recurring job creating costumes for the various stage plays and musicals that came to the Fox. She not only made the outfits in advance, but she had to be on-site during all the performances in case an actor ripped his or her costume in the middle of a show. With no one else to care for her young daughter, Granny had no choice but to take my mother with her every night. That meant my mother spent much of her early years backstage at one of the Southeast's premier theaters, watching show after show, completely surrounded by music, dancing, costumes, elaborate sets, and cheering crowds.

All this artistic exposure had quite an impact on Mom, and no one was surprised when she took a strong interest in dancing. Granny couldn't afford dance lessons, but she still came up with a solution. Because she had developed a reputation for her performance costumes, many of the dance schools around town hired her to create the costumes for their dance recitals. Along with those connections and relationships came plenty of offers for free dance lessons for the master seamstress's little girl. Besides, Mom

was a natural talent and cute as a button. Any teacher would have been thrilled to have her represent their school!

Like she said herself in the introduction, Mom went on to win all kinds of local dance competitions as a child. She won a small cash prize and a ribbon pretty much any time she stepped on the stage, and she was even named the best dancer in Atlanta at just six years old. I still have her old, tiny tap and ballet shoes. It's hard for me to imagine my mother's feet slipping into these little shoes, but every time they did, Mom won an award. I'd give anything to be able to see the smile on her face as the crowd cheered her on back then.

At home, though, things weren't always as happy. By the time the Depression hit, Mom and Granny were living with Granny's parents. Any money Mom won from her dancing competitions went straight to supporting the family. Child or not, it was all hands on deck back then. Mom's grandfather—Granny's dad— was the only man in Mom's life for her first ten years or so. He was a good man and did his best to support his family, but the Depression hit him hard (as it did with most men of the time). He had a difficult time finding steady work and found himself relying on Granny's seamstress income to keep the family above water. I'm sure that took a toll on him.

Mom, on the other hand, was loving the spotlight as a performer. Word spread about the little singer and dancer, and Granny started getting calls from several businesses and churches, wanting Mom to perform. Granny agreed more often than not, and she sent her little girl off in a car with total strangers several times a month. It seems unthinkable today. I have a hard time believing this was normal behavior even back in the 1920s, but Mom made it home safely every time. Looking back on those days, Mom once said, "I suppose

anything could have happened to me, but I had a heavenly Father looking out for me." She certainly did.

That idea of a heavenly Father was a cornerstone for Mom throughout her entire life. She first heard of a God who loved her and cared for her when she was five years old. Family friends had invited her to church, and she was amazed by the idea of a heavenly Father who wanted to walk with her throughout her life. She accepted Him immediately and ran home to tell her mother all about Him. Soon after, the little five-year-old evangelist led her mother to the Lord. Years later, Granny and Mom were baptized together. The two abandoned girls found peace and joy in the arms of the One who'd never leave.

Later in life, Mom found herself speaking to crowds at different churches and Chick-fil-A events, and she almost always spoke of her father *and* her Father. Many times, I heard her say, "I grew up without an earthly father. He abandoned me and my mother when I was three months old, so I never knew him. I never saw him alive again after that." Then she'd always perk up and say, "But that's alright; don't feel sorry for me! Because I have a perfect heavenly Father. I talk to Him just like I'm talking to you now. We discuss things all day, every day. I don't regret not having an earthly father at all. In fact, I think I'm pretty privileged. When I talk to some people, they may say their father wasn't great or that he did *this* or didn't do *that*, and they often ended up hurt and confused by his actions. Not me. I have a perfect Father—one that has only ever loved me, supported me, and protected me. So, don't feel bad for me. I sure don't!"

She wasn't kidding when she said she talked to God all day just like she would to you or me. My mother enjoyed an almost ninety-year, unending, ongoing conversation with the Lord. She

talked to Him *all the time*. And she talked to Him out loud, just like she was entertaining a friend over coffee. Growing up, we'd always hear Mom in the other room doing chores, studying her Bible, or sitting at the piano just chatting away. One of my favorite things was to hear my mother talking and laughing when she was in a room all by herself because I knew she really *wasn't* all by herself. She was talking to her Father with the same joy and affection that I had when talking to mine.

She also wasn't kidding when she said she never saw her earthly father *alive* again. She did, however, see him after his death. She was in her early forties when she got the call. A distant cousin she hardly knew called to let her know that her father had passed away. My brothers and I were quite young at the time, so I don't remember much about it. I do remember thinking how strange it must be to hear that your father died but to have no memories of him at all. I doubt she even really knew what he looked like. He left home in 1923 just after her birth, and photographs weren't nearly as common as they are today, so I'm not sure that she ever even had a picture of him. For whatever reason, though, she chose to go to the funeral.

She dressed my brothers and me up in our nice clothes and she and Dad drove us to Alabama for the service. I can't imagine how hard it must have been to walk into a crowd of people under those circumstances. What do you say to the people who actually knew him and loved him? How do you introduce yourself without inadvertently speaking ill of the dead? What if you strike up a conversation with someone only to find out later he or she was a half-brother or half-sister you never knew about? Mom didn't let that stop her, though. Her earthly father had died, and she wanted one chance—her *only* chance—to see him and to pay her respects.

Mom and Dad got us children squared away on a pew, then Dad took Mom's hand and they walked down the aisle toward the open casket. There, laying in the box was the cold, lifeless body of the man who gave my mother life. The man who hurt my Granny more deeply than I can imagine, leaving her to raise a baby alone. The man who ensured my mother would grow up without the strong hand of a godly earthly father. So many emotions must have welled up in my mother at that moment as she stood there looking on the face of her father for the first time in her life. Among the many emotions she no doubt experienced, I think the most overriding sensation was perhaps the most surprising one: forgiveness. This man was just that: *a man*. He was weak and flawed and just as deeply in need of salvation as she was. He needed what Mom had always had—a heavenly Father to lead and guide him through the maze of life. She had prayed often that he found that peace before he died. Standing there beside his remains, she could only hope that he did.

As strange and emotional as that funeral must have been for her, it didn't change anything for my mother. It didn't raise new pains or bring up new questions about *who* she was or *whose* she was. She was still what she'd always been. In the words of her favorite hymn, she was "A Child of the King." She'd often sing that classic throughout the day, reminding herself in song that she was wholly known and wholly loved by her heavenly Father. I can still hear her sweet voice gently cracking with age as she sang:

> My Father is rich in houses and lands,
> He holdeth the wealth of the world in His hands!
> Of rubies and diamonds, of silver and gold,
> His coffers are full, He has riches untold.

I'm a child of the King,
A child of the King;
With Jesus my Savior,
I'm a child of the King.

My Father's own Son the Savior of men,
Once wandered on earth as the poorest of them;
But now He is pleading our pardon on high,
That we may be His when He comes by and by.

I'm a child of the King,
A child of the King;
With Jesus my Savior,
I'm a child of the King.

I once was an outcast stranger on earth,
A sinner by choice, and an alien by birth,
But I've been adopted, my name's written down,
An heir to a mansion, a robe, and a crown.

I'm a child of the King,
A child of the King;
With Jesus my Savior,
I'm a child of the King.[2]

Throughout her entire life—into her sixties, seventies, eighties, and even her nineties—Mom never stopped seeing herself as a child of the King. A *child* of the King. She knew that she'd never

---

2 "A Child of the King," Words: Hattie E. Buell, 1877. Music: John B. Sumner, 1877. Public Domain.

gain enough life experience or wisdom to make her any more than a child before her heavenly Father, and she was content with that.

I cannot think of my mother without thinking about her relationship with God. It's actually odd for me to use the word *God* here, because Mom rarely did. She didn't say *God* or *Lord* very often; it was always *Father*. She certainly didn't think there was anything wrong with using the other terms, but, at least in her case, calling Him *God* just wasn't personal enough. I think she saw it like a child calling her earthly father by his business title. If you were the daughter of the president of the United States, for example, would you call him *Mr. President*, or would you just fall in his arms and call him *Daddy*? For my mother, the answer was clear: she was His child, and He was her Father—period.

As long as her perfect Father was with her, holding her hand and lifting her up, she knew she could do anything, go anywhere, accomplish any goal, and overcome any obstacle. She felt as safe in His arms at ninety-two as I did in my own father's arms at two. She always knew He was there with her—there *for* her—no matter what. With that kind of assurance, she knew she'd never be alone. And she never was.

CHAPTER 2

The Courtship of Jeannette McNeil

y parents had an amazing relationship; everyone who saw them together commented on how connected and in love they seemed. I have a photograph of them in their nineties sitting in a Chick-fil-A booth sharing a single soda with two straws. The image makes me smile every time I see it. It perfectly captures who they were *to* each other and *with* each other. That picture makes it easy to imagine them sitting at the counter of the Dwarf Grill doing the same thing sixty years earlier.

Looking back on their life together, I can't help but see the Lord's hand on them every step of the way. Even from the very beginning, they had so much working against them. Neither came from a household that demonstrated what a healthy, godly marriage looked like. The only man who'd been a constant presence in my mother's life before she married Dad was her grandfather. She never even met her own father, let alone had any kind of relationship with him. Her mother never remarried, and Mom had no brothers or sisters to grow up with. It was just Mom, her mother, and her grandparents. She really had no training at all on how to be a godly wife. I honestly don't know how she pulled it off—but she did.

Dad, on the other hand, came from a big family of seven children. His parents stayed married, but life was hard for them during the Great Depression. For a while, Dad and his brother Ben were the primary breadwinners for the family. My father was just fourteen years old at the time, and Ben was even younger. They paid most of the family bills with money they earned from their paper routes. A few years later, at age eighteen, Dad was drafted into the Army during World War II. He served with honor for six years and came home in 1945 to find work and start making a living. The next year, he and Ben opened the Dwarf Grill (later renamed Dwarf House) with just four tables and ten stools at the lunch counter. Their first day's business receipts totaled $58.20. It wasn't the most auspicious beginning, but it was the start they needed to get what would become Chick-fil-A off the ground!

Mom and Dad knew each other as children. They went to the same middle school and junior high, but Mom didn't remember interacting with Dad much back then. Their lives were always intertwined, though. In fact, as Mom mentioned in the introduction, she even traveled as a young girl with Dad's sister Agnes one summer as the musical guest for Agnes's husband's church revival services. Mom was so young and tiny back then! The only way she could see over the podium was by standing in a chair and leaning over to the microphone. I wish I could have seen that! At the end of each week, Agnes and her husband, Dock, drove Mom back home for the weekend. Their first stop upon getting back into town, though, was the Cathy house. Many of the churches where Dock preached could only pay him in chickens and produce, so he and Agnes would drop those goodies off at the Cathy's boarding house on their way home. That "revival income" was used to feed Mrs. Cathy's boarders during the week.

Mom waited in the backseat while Dock and Agnes unloaded the car at the Cathy's house. Oftentimes, she'd see two little boys— Truett and Ben—playing on the front porch of the boarding house. It's funny to imagine God looking down on that little girl—who probably didn't give that boy a second thought at the time—knowing the pair would one day become husband and wife and spend nearly every day together for sixty-five years!

Mom and Dad's lives crisscrossed over their teen years. They didn't see each other much because Dad was at an all-boy high school and Mom was at an all-girl high school. Plus, Dad spent most of his free time working to support his family before being drafted into the Army right out of high school. They did see each other a bit through their families' shared love of music, though. Mom was a natural talent with singing and playing many different instruments, and Dad's brothers enjoyed playing guitar. Several times during those early years, Mom was invited over to the Cathy house to sing and play with Dad's brothers. Even though Dad wasn't musically gifted himself (something that frustrated him throughout his life), he enjoyed the opportunities to see the pretty girl from two doors down. As my brother Bubba often says, "I think Dad was stricken with a terrible case of love at first sight. No other girl ever compared."

While he was serving during the war, Mom, like most women on the home front during that time, went to work. She settled into a nice job at a government accounting office and enjoyed her work, but she struggled with a persistent call to serve the Lord in a different way. One night while at a summer church retreat in North Carolina, Mom heard a definite call to Christian service that she simply could not ignore. She later mentioned this to her church ladies' group and was thrilled when they offered to send her to college and seminary. College wasn't that unusual for women in the early 1940s, but seminary was a different matter. Her boldness in leaving home and heading to New Orleans all alone to study God's Word and prepare for ministry service has always been a powerful encouragement to me.

Mom was still working on her seminary degree in New Orleans when Dad returned from the Army. Around that time, Mom's mother (my Granny) made a recital dress for the daughter of another Cathy sister, Gladys. As Granny and Gladys chatted one day, Gladys asked how Mom was doing. Granny bragged that she was off at seminary and said she'd be home for Easter. That was the opening Matchmaker Gladys needed! She suggested that her brother Truett should come pick Mom up while she was home from school and take her to Gladys's house for dinner so they all could catch up. A few weeks later, my parents had their first official date at my aunt's house. They all had a good time, but Mom had to get back to school. Dad couldn't stop thinking about her after that, though.

A while later, Dad came up with a scheme to see her again. He struck up a conversation with Granny and asked if she'd ever visited Mom in New Orleans. They talked about the sights and unique experiences of New Orleans a bit, and then Dad—out of the goodness of his heart, I'm sure—offered to drive Granny down to New Orleans to visit her daughter. And if Dad got to take Mom out for dinner while they were there, well, why not? They picked a weekend to surprise my mother at school—and surprise her they did. Mom was thrilled to see her mother and happy to see Dad, but there was an unexpected kink in Dad's master plan: Mom already had a date scheduled for that night! Never wanting to break a commitment, Mom went off on her date while Dad entertained *her mother* in New Orleans. I'm sure it wasn't the magical evening Dad had envisioned, but it was enough. They got to spend a little time together before Dad and Granny headed home, and, as Dad has long admitted, he was quite taken with the beautiful seminarian. He often said of those days, "I always either wanted to marry Shirley Temple or Jeannette McNeil!"

Their courtship began in earnest when Mom returned home after completing her seminary studies in 1947. Dad was neck-deep in restaurant responsibilities at that time, as he and Ben were putting everything they had into building a successful business. Dad even rented a room in the house next door to the Dwarf Grill so the employees could come knock on his window if he was needed in the middle of the night. He worked so hard all day, six days a week, that, when they did go out during the week, there was a good chance he'd fall asleep! Sundays, though, were different. The restaurant was closed on Sundays (something he and Ben committed to from the very beginning), so Dad got a chance to rest and enjoy the day with Mom. They'd go to church together and then stop by the empty restaurant to check on things. While they were there, they'd share a soda at the counter and listen to the jukebox as they talked away the afternoon. Those slow, lazy Sundays meant everything to them. I can't tell you how often I heard both of them talk about those days with the unmistakable glimmer of love in their far-off stares.

Dad eventually proposed on Georgia's beautiful Lookout Mountain. It couldn't have been a surprise for my mother. She knew how much he loved her, and she knew how much they both strove to make the most of every opportunity together. It was only natural for them to marry and begin spending a lifetime of opportunities as husband and wife. Mom, however, didn't give him an answer right away. I can just picture my poor father on one knee overlooking that majestic scenic view waiting desperately for *some* answer to the question she allowed to hang in the air. But Mom needed to be sure—absolutely sure—that this was her Father's plan for her life. She refused to go through a failed marriage like her mother did. As much as she loved my dad, she wouldn't let herself rush into it. Not until she prayed about it *a lot*.

A few days later, while sitting at the lunch counter at the restaurant sharing a Coke and listening to the jukebox, Mom gave her answer. Of course, she said yes. Yes to a lifelong adventure. Yes to becoming Jeannette Cathy. Yes to more than six decades of early morning breakfasts, farm adventures, missed dinners, building a business, hosting Chick-fil-A dinners, and an endless stream of visitors and unexpected dinner guests. Yes to three children, twelve grandchildren, and supporting a whole host of foster children through their ministry endeavors. Yes to a long, rich, incredibly blessed life with her best friend, partner, and soul mate.

They were married on September 19, 1948, at West End Baptist Church. My father's sister Myrtle—a fantastic cook and businessperson in her own right—catered the event. And my Granny, of course, made Mom's wedding gown. After a successful career as a seamstress, this gown was her masterpiece; my mother looked absolutely stunning. In fact, when I got engaged many years later, I asked Mom if I could see her wedding gown. We pulled it down from the attic and Mom told me to try it on. It fit like a glove, just as though Granny had made it for *me*.

Standing there stunned at the perfect fit, I told Mom I loved the dress and asked if I could wear it on my wedding. In typical, humble Jeannette Cathy fashion, she replied, "Oh, Trudy, you don't want to wear this. It's so old! Let's get you something new to wear." I wouldn't hear of it. I knew there was no other dress on earth that would mean more to me than the one my mother wore to marry my father. Even though she resisted at first, she finally gave in and said yes. I was so proud to walk down the aisle wearing my mother's wedding gown. I felt like she was clothing me in more than a dress. She was also clothing me in her prayers that I might enjoy the same blessed marriage she and Dad had modeled for me all those years.

We can all only hope to have the kind of intimate, friendly, playful, loving, prayer-filled marriage I saw in my parents. It's the highest standard I could imagine, and one my husband, John, and I still strive to live up to more than forty years later.

CHAPTER 3

Eddie White

Eddie White is one of our family's oldest and dearest friends. Our relationship goes back more than seventy years—long before I was ever even born. Eddie was twelve years old when Mom and Dad first got to know him. His cousin worked at Dad's restaurant and asked if Eddie could start working there too. Even though Eddie was younger than the other employees, he was big for his age and carried himself with a maturity far beyond his years. From the moment he came in for an impromptu job interview with my father, it was clear Eddie was a special young man. Dad gave him a job on the spot. Eddie didn't know it at the time, but his entire life changed at that moment. And, in a way, so did ours.

Eddie was a bright child and excelled in school, but the reason he worked is that his family needed the extra income he brought in. The year was 1948, and it seemed that African American families like his had to work twice as hard for half as much back then. Fortunately for his family, Eddie was an extremely hard worker. Dad put him to work immediately, and he did everything around the restaurant. He washed dishes, cleared tables, kept up the grounds around the Dwarf House, and, over time, became the Dwarf's best cook and on-site butcher. My father thought the world of Eddie—an opinion my mother shared as soon as she met him.

Eddie once told me how disarming my mother was to him. For example, one day while he was in the back of the restaurant washing dishes, she went back to help. There they were, side by side, with their hands splashing in and out of the same dirty water, working together and talking through the lunchtime rush. My mom was in her late twenties then, and she and Dad were newly-weds who spent most of their time in the restaurant. That meant the employees around them, including twelve-year-old Eddie, were quickly becoming part of their little family.

Mom loved to chat with him. She asked about his family, his friends, his favorite classes at school, and his plans as he grew up. Despite the difference in age and, let's face it, the different social standing (this *was* the late 1940s, after all) Eddie never felt out of place with my mother. He was quite the conversationalist, and that suited my mother just fine. She loved to chat too! Those workday gab sessions over the sink full of dirty dishes became cherished time for both of them as they developed a sweet, loving relationship of mutual respect.

Despite his comfort level with my mother, Eddie was still keenly aware of the times he was living in. Race may not have been an issue for my parents, but young men like Eddie had to be careful about what they said and did in racially mixed envi-ronments. It hurts me to even type those words, but, as Eddie has often said, times were much different back then. That's what made his relationship with my parents so special; no matter what anyone else said or did to Eddie, he knew that Truett and Jeannette Cathy would stand beside him and support him.

I sat down with Eddie recently to talk about their relationship, and he told me some great stories about how my parents impacted his life. One of the things that stands out the most to him is how my mother treated him outside the restaurant. He wasn't just an employee to my parents; he was a trusted friend. Mom not only talked to him and made him feel welcome inside the safe confines of the Dwarf House. No, she had that same openness and twinkle-eyed charm and affection for him no matter where they were or who else was around.

There were several times when Eddie helped Mom around the house with the yard work and other odd jobs. One day in particular, he had spent the morning cutting the grass and trimming the hedges. He remembers my mother coming out several times to check on him. "Eddie, you aren't getting too hot, are you?" "Eddie, don't forget to take a break when you need it. I don't want to wear you out!" "Eddie, can I get you a glass of tea?" He felt like part of the family that morning, just doing his part to take care of the home. However, as lunchtime approached, Mom did something that stretched even Eddie's comfort level.

"Mrs. Cathy came out and asked me if I was hungry for lunch, and I certainly was," he recalls. "I was thinking she'd just grab something and bring it out to me, but that's not what she did. She went inside for a while and then came out saying, 'Hey, Eddie. Lunch is ready. I set a place for you at my table. Come on in and eat!'"

"This was sort of strange for me," he continues. "You have to remember, this was the early fifties, and times were vastly different then. For Mrs. Cathy to not only fix me lunch but to serve it to me herself at her kitchen table inside her home . . . it really drove home the fact that this was a fantastically different family."

He also remembers a time, years later, when my parents saved him from quitting school. He was a junior in high school at that point, and things had gotten especially hard for his family. Up to that point, Eddie had worked in the restaurant part time during the school year and full time during the summers. At this critical time, however, he was considering leaving school and working full-time year-round. Eddie was the oldest of seven children. His father already worked two jobs, and his mother worked as much as she could while also caring for seven little ones and their home. Even though he'd been working since age twelve, Eddie felt like he needed to do more to serve his family. The only option, he thought, was to quit school and work during the day.

Eddie sat down with my father to discuss his plan, and Dad was not a fan of the idea. Eddie excelled in school and had big dreams for his future. He'd always talked about being a doctor or an educator, and my parents couldn't bear the idea of Eddie giving up those dreams and spending the rest of his life in the Dwarf House. Dad talked it over with Mom, and they agreed that—as much as it was in their power—they were not going to let Eddie quit school. My dad even met with Eddie's father to discuss other options. Mom and Dad were willing to give Eddie as many hours as he could work and support him any way they could, providing he stayed in school and graduated. Eddie and his father agreed, and they all celebrated Eddie's high school graduation a little over a year later.

Eddie's incredible work ethic and sharp mind resulted in a full four-year scholarship to Morris Brown College in Atlanta. His family's financial troubles still weighed heavily on his mind, however, and he decided they needed him more than ever. He finally went full-time with the Dwarf House and decided to decline the scholarship and put college off for a while. He worked pretty much every day that year. The restaurant was closed on Sundays, but Eddie still came in on Sunday afternoons to chop meat and get things ready for the week. He'd become the Dwarf House's resident butcher by then and gave his all to his job—and then some. One day while chopping some beef, Eddie's finger slipped into the slicer and was cut off at the knuckle. If you're curious how hard a worker he was, just listen to this: Eddie was back at work the next day. "I missed half a day for half my finger," he jokes. Clearly, my parents had an incredible friend, partner, and team member in Eddie White!

Because he'd become such a beloved fixture of the restaurant by then, my mother and the other waitresses got together to figure out how to help Eddie finally get to college. He'd given so much for his family and for the business, and they wanted to find a way to give back to him. Someone—either my mother or my Aunt Gladys—came up with the idea to put a gallon jug on the counter next to the cash register. As people paid for their food, they'd say, "Did you enjoy your meal? If so, the guy who cooked it is trying to go to college, and anything you drop in this jug will help him get there!" So, for the next six months, that gallon jug sat on the counter and collected tips dedicated to Eddie's college education. When it was time for Eddie to register for classes, he and my parents took the jug off the counter and counted all the money. They had collected enough for half a year's tuition, which Eddie thought was pretty good. Mom and Dad didn't think it was enough, though. So, they dropped a check in the jug for the other half of Eddie's first-year's tuition, giving him what was probably the first ever Chick-fil-A college scholarship!

Before classes began, my parents wanted to make sure Eddie had everything he needed for a great start. That meant Eddie needed to do a little shopping. Mom and Dad knew neither Eddie nor his family could afford nice clothes for college, so they set him up with a couple of great outfits from the nicest men's store in Atlanta at the time. They made all the arrangements, and Eddie got the full treatment—from his custom-fit blazer down to his dress socks! Later, when he came by the Dwarf House to show off his new clothes, my mother doted on him like crazy. "Oh, Eddie! You look so sharp! You're going to be the best-dressed guy at college!" And he probably was.

Eddie went on to have a fantastic career as a well-respected educator in an Atlanta area school system. He spent nearly forty years teaching and then serving as the assistant superintendent before he retired in the 1990s. He remained close to my parents through the decades, always catching up with my mother whenever they ran into each other. The two of them always seemed to slip right back into the same easy, casual conversations they once had standing over the dirty dishes at the Dwarf House decades earlier.

Eddie's close connection to our family was accentuated even more in 2010, when a new K–8 school prepared to open in Atlanta's Clayton County. The school board was charged with naming the school, and they wanted to name it after someone in the community. After narrowing the long list of names, the board came down to two names as potential honorees: Eddie White and Truett Cathy. Eddie quipped, "Quite remarkable company to be in, don't you think?" It sure is—and I know my dad thought so too. To all our joy, they decided to name the school the Eddie J. White K–8 Academy. Even after sixty-two long years, my mom and dad could not have been prouder of him or more excited to show their support and encouragement. When Eddie cut the ribbon at the school's opening ceremony in 2010, my parents were right there cheering him on.

"The Cathys were like family to me," Eddie recalls. The weight of those words isn't lost on him. In a time when racial barriers kept many people apart, Eddie White and my parents enjoyed a rich, loving, lifelong friendship. "Race simply didn't matter inside that restaurant," Eddie says. "We were all like family, and that started with Mr. and Mrs. Cathy."

It always makes me laugh to hear him call Mom, "Mrs. Cathy." You'd think that, after a close relationship of nearly seventy years, he would have gotten comfortable calling her by her first name! He never did. "I can't think of a single time when I ever called her *Jeannette*," he says. "It just didn't feel respectful enough. She was a real encourager to me all my life. Whatever I was doing, she was right there saying, 'You can do it. You can be whatever you want to be. We are proud of you. Let us know if there is anything we can do to help you.' And she meant it."

CHAPTER 4

The Great Bee Debacle
of 1957

In 1957, our family moved from our little house on Sylvan Road near Dad's restaurant to a farm out in the country. It was wonderful! Mom and Dad had both been raised in Atlanta and had always dreamed about having a big piece of property to enjoy. Dad had limited exposure to farm life when he was very young; his father farmed cotton until a boll weevil infestation destroyed his business when Dad was just four years old. Mom, however, was a complete city girl with no farm experience beyond occasional visits in her childhood. I think they were caught off guard by how much work it took to keep a farm up and running.

The 262-acre property was massive. I was only two when we moved there, and it seemed like the hills and pastures rolled on forever. A long dirt driveway connected the house to the country road at the edge of the property. Cows wallowed in a retention pond a couple of hundred yards from the house, and a dark and murky swamp—forbidden territory to us as children—hemmed us in from the back of the lot. As expansive as the property was, the little farmhouse we lived in was tiny. It was a small, two-bedroom home with one bathroom. My brothers and I—ages four, three, and two—shared one of the bedrooms while our parents took the other. I'm sure it felt cramped at times, but we didn't mind. All we had to do was step outside to have all the room we needed to run, play, and explore the seemingly endless property.

Dad still worked at the restaurant from sunup to sundown, of course, so Mom took the brunt of the farm-life culture shock in those early years. We'd always lived close to Dad's restaurant and had plenty of friends and neighbors right outside our door to talk to, play with, and help with anything that came up. But now, we were isolated on a patch of farmland all by ourselves. I didn't appreciate at the time how difficult (or downright scary) that must have been for my mother. Looking back on it now, I can't imagine the strength and courage it must have taken for her to face each day on a farm full of cows and other animals with no farmhand or easy access to help in an emergency. And let's not forget that she also had three children under the age of five running around. I'm sure it felt more like a zoo than a farm most days!

Mom often told me about the moment she realized she was all alone out there. We had been on the farm for two or three months. Dad was at work, and something happened with the cows that really panicked my mother. Of course, she had no idea how to solve the problem. All she knew was that she was facing an urgent situation and needed immediate help. Remember, this was 1957; there were no cell phones, pagers, or 911 service. And there certainly wasn't a *farm-emergency hotline* to call. This is the kind of situation that once would have sent her knocking on a neighbor's door for help. The problem was, though . . . there were no neighbors anymore.

"I ran down to the edge of the property," she told me, "and I looked up and down the road. Nothing. So, I climbed up on top of the fence and yelled at the top of my voice, 'HELP! HELP! Somebody, help me!' Nothing. Nothing but the cows mooing and the birds chirping."

"There I was, on the farm all by myself with three young children and an emergency I didn't think I could handle. I climbed off the fence and talked to the only other person around. I said, 'Okay, Father. It's just you and me. Whatever comes up around here, we'll have to find a way to solve it together.' And we did. From that point on, whenever there was an emergency on the farm, I knew who to call: the Lord."

Something happened to my mother that day. She'd always been smart and resourceful, but that experience standing on the fence showed her she really was the chief problem solver, repairman, plumber, electrician, and farmhand of the property. The farm was so far off the beaten path that she even had trouble scheduling professionals to come to the house for most routine issues. She always joked, "I can't get a workman to come out here for love or money!" In fact, it was decades before she had any consistent help on the farm outside the house, and that was only because she and Dad hired on-site employees to take care of things. Even into her sixties, it was pretty common for us to come into the house and see a vacuum or appliance laying in the floor in pieces as she worked to fix whatever was broken. "Don't touch anything!" she'd say. "I know how to get it back together!" And she almost always did.

While she and the Lord had a stellar track record of taking care of most of the little issues that happened around the farm, there was one mishap that she was especially ill-equipped to handle. It was our first year on the farm, and we had settled in nicely after a few bumps. Mom even had a little help with the housework at this point—a sixteen-year-old girl named Annette who came one or two days a week. One day, Mom picked Annette up for work and gave her just about the worst marching orders she'd ever heard: "Annette, we've got to go get the honey out of the beehives, and we've got to do it ourselves. There's nobody else out here that can help us."

You see, the previous owners of the farm had kept bees for honey and had six large beehives on the other side of the property, far from the house. Someone had recently told Mom about them and suggested she empty them out. Much to Annette's dismay, today was the day to harvest some honey.

Of course, Mom had no idea *how* to get the honey out of the hives. She didn't even know how to safely approach the swarms of bees without getting stung to death. However, she didn't waste time trying to find a professional beekeeper to make the drive out to the country to help. She'd already learned her lesson on the fencepost; she knew she was on her own. And this time, Annette was along for the ride.

When I say *along for the ride*, I mean that quite literally. Since the beehives were on the other side of the property, Mom and Annette had to take the truck. Fortunately, before they drove off, they covered up as well as they could with long sleeves, long gloves, and hats with veils over their faces. Covered up like country mummies, the two ladies set off to confront the bees.

Annette's face dropped when they found them. I'm sure Mom was worried, too, but she didn't let Annette see her hesitation.

Someone in that situation had to act like they knew what they were doing! The problem was, they didn't. Mom was just as clueless as Annette; they had no idea how to move the hives, get the bees out of the way, and extract the heaping pools of honey. But that didn't stop them from trying.

The pair nervously crept up to the six large beehives as a stream of bees buzzed in and out of their sticky insect condos. With as much confidence as she could muster, Mom reached out and took the lid off one of the hives. Looking inside, she saw what seemed like a million bees working away, tending to their rich stores of honey. The sound took her by surprise. She said it sounded like a thousand little buzz saws grinding away in a flurry of activity. Of course, some curious drones flew up and out the top when she took the lid off, but most of the bees stayed at their posts inside the hive. There was literally an army standing between my mother and the sticky treasure she'd come to collect, and she had to figure out how to rob the honey bank without upsetting all the pesky little soldiers inside.

For some reason, Mom planned to extract the honey from the hives back at the house, so her first goal was to simply move the hives from one place to the other. So, the two makeshift beekeepers lifted each hive by its frame and, slowly and carefully, loaded each of the six beehives onto the bed of the pickup truck. Honey started dripping everywhere. The truck had become a buzzing, frightening, sticky mess, but the first step of their master plan was complete! They got back in the truck and started driving toward the house. At that point, Mom noticed in the rearview mirror that a *lot* of bees were coming out of the hives to see what all the commotion was. In fact, the bed of the truck was *full* of bees. Looking over at her nervous partner in crime, Mom said, "You know, I don't think I want all those bees inside my house.

We've got to get the bees completely out of the hives before we take them in. What to do, what to do?"

She joked later, "The Lord always tells me what to do in these situations, you know. But I'm not sure if this was really one of *His* ideas."

I'm going to go out on a limb and say the idea she came up with was definitely *not* divinely inspired. Turning away from the house, Mom headed for what we called *the circle*. It was a corral we used as a horse-riding rink beside our backyard, located at the end of a path our tractor had worn into the dirt. Looking over to Annette, Mom said, "Let's go over to the circle. I'll drive *real fast*. That way, we'll *outrun the bees*. They can't fly as fast as we can drive—everybody knows that!"

So, there's my mother, completely covered head to toe in her makeshift beekeeper gear doing donuts in a fenced-in horse rink with six giant beehives rattling around in the back of the pickup and a faint cloud of angry bees trailing behind her. If only there was a video!

She circled the truck until she couldn't see any more bees in the rearview mirror. Turning to her now-terrified and motion-sick teenaged helper, Mom said, "I don't see them anymore! Quick, let's get back to the house before the bees can catch us!" With that, she floored the accelerator and raced back across the dirt path to the house. Dirt, gravel, bees, and honey flew through the air as she wheeled around to the carport and backed the truck up to the house. Still trying to outrun and outwit the bees, Mom and Annette jumped out of the car and unloaded all six beehives as quickly as they could—right inside the house. The washer and dryer were just inside the door, so they piled the beehives in the laundry room, certain the dirty containers were full of nothing but golden, delicious honey at this point.

Sadly, they were wrong. Sure, the hives were full of honey. But they were also still full of bees. And by this point, the bees were . . . displeased.

With a squadron of bees taking offensive positions all throughout the house and every inch of her laundry room covered in raw honey, Mom did something she almost never did: she gave up. She and Annette loaded the beehives back in the truck and drove them away. We never saw them again. The pair spent the rest of the afternoon scraping goo off the washing machine and swatting bees away from napping children, all in a desperate attempt to erase all evidence of "The Great Bee Debacle of 1957" before my father came home from work. They were only mildly successful.

More than sixty years later, our whole family still giggles anytime someone opens up a jar of honey. Homegrown honey may be tasty, but Mom decided that day it was definitely not worth the effort.

CHAPTER 5

Mr. Zach's Unexpected Introduction

When my parents moved to the farm, they knew they had a lot to learn about rural farm living. Again, neither had ever worked on a farm or spent much time on one growing up, so they both knew it would take a lot of work to get things (and keep things) up and running. They were prepared for that; neither Mom nor Dad were ever scared of a little hard work. One thing that surprised them, though, was the constant stream of strangers who trespassed on their property every day. It was the weirdest thing. If Mom needed help with something, there was no one to be found; she'd be stuck in an emergency all alone with no one to come to her aid. However, if she happened to look out her window at any other point during the day, there was a good chance she'd see someone she didn't know walking across the field on the way to the Flint River on the back side of the property. "Where were these burly guys when I was screaming for help on the fencepost?" she often wondered aloud.

The problem was that Mom and Dad's 262 acres included some of the best hunting and fishing spots in the area. Their farm had sat vacant for years before they bought it, and all the locals had gotten used to walking, hiking, hunting, fishing, and exploring all over it. Can you imagine being a young woman alone on a giant piece of property in the middle of nowhere with three small children—two still in diapers—and seeing a rough-looking, rifle-packing outdoorsman coming toward your house? That's what my mother had to put up with every day. It became quite a problem. It's not that the locals were intentionally being rude or willfully disregarding private property; it's just that everyone in the area had gotten used to the property sitting vacant. Once people finally understood our family had moved in, things settled down and the trespassers dwindled off. Almost.

In those early days on the farm, Mom was still figuring out how to take care of three children under four years old *and* the house *and* the farm mostly by herself. By the time the trespassing problem all but dried up, she was getting into a groove and had things running fairly smoothly. She had her daily routines, which always included getting up early and fixing Dad a good breakfast before he left for the restaurant. No matter how early he had to leave, Mom always got up a little earlier to send him out the door with a full stomach. Plus, she treasured those breakfasts with her overworked husband. No matter what the day held, no matter how far into the evenings Dad would have to work, Mom knew she got to start each day with her two great loves: her heavenly Father and her loving husband. As far as I know, she rarely missed a morning with either of them.

One morning after Dad had left for work, Mom turned her attention to the breakfast dishes. While scraping bacon grease off the frying pan and wiping jelly off Dad's plate, she was interrupted by . . . well, let's just call it a diaper emergency. Don't blame me; I was barely two years old at the time! She scooped me and my brother Bubba up and took us back to our bedroom for a quick cleanup and diaper change. So far, it was a perfectly normal day on the Cathy farm. But that was about to change.

Mom finished up with us, washed up, and made her way back to the kitchen. As she rounded the corner through the kitchen door, she stopped dead in her tracks and her jaw hit the floor. A strange man was standing in her kitchen. He was an older gentleman, dirty, and covered in well-worn overalls. A million questions flooded her mind in an instant. *Who is this? What do I do? Where do I go? Where are my children?* Unable to articulate any of those questions into any language known to man, she did what any self-respecting woman in her position would do: she screamed. Loudly. Her shrill shriek filled the house and echoed across the property. It was a scream unlike any she'd ever released before. It startled cows and sent birds flying for at least a mile. It also scared to death the intruder standing in her kitchen.

"I'm sorry! I'm sorry!" he cried. "It's okay. I'm your neighbor!" Mother still kept her distance as he explained, "I am so sorry, ma'am. My name is Zach Mitchell, and I live way down the road. I was cutting through your property just now, and I heard the water running in your kitchen. You must have left the faucet going in the sink when you walked off. I didn't want it to flood your kitchen, so I just ran in to shut it off for you. I never meant to scare you!"

My mother, always a city girl, wasn't accustomed to this level of neighborly . . . *involvement*. It's a wonder she didn't beat him over the head with the dirty frying pan! He spoke kindly, though, and she couldn't help but believe he was simply trying to help (even though he should have knocked before letting himself into the kitchen).

Believe it or not, this dramatic incident was the beginning of a wonderful friendship between my parents and the Mitchells. Neighbors were few and far between out on the farm in those days, so Mom was happy to make a local connection—especially one who didn't hesitate to help out when he saw something wrong. Dad eventually hired "Mr. Zach," as we called him, as a handyman around the farm. He'd come around from time to time to help feed the cows, mend broken fences, and take care of little odds and ends around the house. One of Mr. Zach's first chores, ironically, was to help Mom and Dad cut off the flow of unwanted traffic across our farm. He wrote out a handmade sign and posted it at the edge of our property, warning all trespassers to "KEP OT!" For the longest time, my brothers and I wondered what "KEP OT" meant. Eventually, my father replaced Mr. Zach's masterpiece with a large metal sign that read, "NO FISHING, NO HUNTING, NO TRESPASSING. DON'T EVEN ASK." As much as my father loved entertaining, even he was fed up with the endless string of unwelcome guests who trekked across their fields every day.

Mr. Zach brought a sense of peace and assurance to my mother, who was still getting used to days alone on the farm. For the first time since they moved to the country, Mom didn't feel so alone out there anymore. She especially took a liking to Mr. Zach's wife, Annie. She looked exactly like the Granny Clampett character from *The Beverly Hillbillies* television show of the 1960s. Mrs. Annie was a tiny elderly woman with her hair pulled back into a tight bun and small wire glasses that sat at the tip of her nose. Like her TV counterpart, she always wore an apron over her modest dress, and her back was always a little hunched over. They were such a sweet couple, and we all grew to love them like family.

The Mitchells were country people in every sense of the word—outhouse and all. They were born in the 1880s and had moved into their little house in 1920. Mr. Zach even slept on the floor because he thought the hard, wooden floor was better for his aching back than the old, lumpy mattress they had. As the couple got older, Mom grew more concerned about their well-being. Their little house was way down the main road, well out of earshot. That was a problem for my mother, because the Mitchells' house had no electricity, no indoor plumbing, and—most importantly for Mom—no telephone service. That meant Mrs. Annie had no way of calling for help if there was an emergency. As far as my mother was concerned, that just wouldn't do.

After talking it over with my father, Mom arranged to have the Mitchell's house wired for electricity and telephone service. They sent crews to their home and took care of all the details and expense. My parents were certainly not wealthy at that point in their lives, but that never stopped them from helping other people whenever and however they could. Sure, it cost a lot of money to fully wire someone else's home, but it was worth it to my mother just for the peace of mind of being able to check on Mrs. Annie whenever she wanted to.

The Mitchells weren't just my parents' friends; my brothers and I loved them too! I remember when we were a little older, we got trail bikes to ride around the farm. Mr. Zach and Mrs. Annie loved riding around on those bikes with us for a quick spin around the property. It was such a sight to see them hanging onto the back of our bikes in their old age, whooping and hollering like teenagers!

Our family remained closely connected to the Mitchells for the rest of their lives. They each died peacefully of old age in their well-loved and well-worn farmhouse. My parents always looked back fondly on the old couple and thought about how peaceful it seemed for them to pass away in the home they loved so much. I've often wondered if my parents thought back on Mr. Zach and Mrs. Annie's final days when they were at the end of their own lives. The Mitchells had given all of us such a wonderful picture of growing old and facing death with grace. That kind of spirit—and love for life—was a gift for which I'll always be thankful.

CHAPTER 6

Pass the Plate, Turn Off the Oven

Sunday mornings were always a busy time for our family. It was the only morning of the week when all five of us—Mom, Dad, Dan, Bubba, and I—were all up and running (and running over each other) at the same time. It was also the only guaranteed time of the week when we were sure to have an outing together, as our family faithfully attended Lovejoy Baptist Church, our wonderful little country church that recently celebrated its centennial celebration, every single week. Attendance was not optional for the Cathy family—not that any of us ever considered skipping. We loved piling in the car and having that protected family time every week.

Our Sunday mornings usually started on Saturday night, when Mom began pre-cooking our big Sunday family meal and

Dad prepared his Sunday School lesson. No matter how busy he was through the years, he never gave up teaching his beloved eighth-grade boys' Sunday School class. It was a priority for him but, given his crazy work schedule, he never got around to preparing his lesson until Saturday night. Mom taught the eighth-grade girls' class, but she always prepared earlier in the week, often while waiting for Dan and me to finish our weekly piano lessons. Dad knew if he didn't prepare his lesson before he went to bed on Saturday, he'd have some trouble. Sunday mornings in our house were *not* made for productive study!

Mom got up early every Sunday to make a big breakfast for us and finish preparing Sunday lunch. I usually woke up to the irresistible aroma of freshly cooked eggs and extra-crispy bacon already on the table while a pot roast simmered in the oven for later. With the day's meals either finished or underway, Mom switched roles from resident chef to harsh taskmaster and timekeeper. She rushed around from child to child making sure everyone was awake, clean, and dressed with nicely combed hair and no obvious stains on our clothes. And, of course, she had to give Dad a few well-placed pokes to keep him on track too. Sunday was *definitely* his day of rest. The Truett Cathy who worked as hard and fast as a raceway pit crew member six days a week was nowhere to be found on Sundays. Mom loved that he made time to relax on Sundays; she just wished he could have relaxed a little faster before church.

Getting us all out the door on time was an honest-to-goodness miracle most Sundays. Mom would beam with pride as we slammed our car doors, and she'd say something like, "We did it! This is the week we'll actually get to church on time!"

Cue the cows.

My goodness, the cows on our farm must have had a giant calendar pinned to the fence. They were well-behaved and orderly

Monday through Saturday but, like clockwork, several cows managed to work their way through the barbed-wire fence on Sundays. And it never happened on the Sundays when we were already running late, mind you. No, these cows almost exclusively took their neighborhood walks on the rare Sundays we were right on schedule. We'd be halfway down the long dirt driveway and notice our cows wandering down the road away from our farm. Any cheerful glimmer of accomplishment on Mom's face was wiped away by the cows' far-off mooing.

Dad would throw the car in park, and he and my brothers would jump out of the car to go Sunday-morning cow-chasing. They'd chase the boneheaded bovines over muddy pastures, through the creek, up the hills, and finally back home to our property. Sitting in the car with my mother as the three victorious ranchers walked back, I saw her shake her head and point back to the house. She couldn't do much to convince Dad to clean up, but she *could* make Dan and Bubba change their now-dirty clothes and muddy shoes. Minutes later, piled back in the car with her sweaty but redressed men in tow, she'd sigh and say, "Well, now we're late. Again. Maybe *next* Sunday. . . ."

Somehow, we all got to our Sunday School classes before the church sent out search parties to look for us. Mom and Dad taught their classes while my brothers and I made our way to ours. Then, when the Sunday School hour was done, Dad had to try wrangling us three children alone in the sanctuary while Mom took her place at the piano. Most Sundays, he had better luck keeping the cows in place than he did keeping three active children quiet and orderly.

Mom played all the music through the service, so she rarely got to sit with us. That didn't mean we never *heard* from her, though. Somewhere around the third verse of the second hymn,

Mom would realize she left the oven on at home. Our house—not to mention our Sunday lunch—was in danger! But what was she to do? This was the 1950s; it's not like she could sneak a quick text message to Dad in the middle of the service. Or could she?

At the end of the song, Mom would grab a pen and a scrap of paper and scribble out a note to my father. She folded it up and, in giant letters on the outside of the note, she wrote "FOR TRUETT." She then placed the note "Truett-side-up" in the offering plate right before the ushers came by to pass the plate. Her note circulated through the first few rows of the sanctuary before finally landing in my dad's lap. It didn't take him long to know he should *always* check the offering plate for a note from my mother. Sure enough, he'd see the note and read it while the three of us giggled. We always knew what it said, because it always said the same thing: "Truett, I left the oven on. You have to run home and turn it off!"

Dad would immediately shoot a look at the three of us that said, "You better behave while I'm gone," and then he'd be off. I can still see him shuffling down the pew with his head down low, as though crouching would render him invisible to others in the congregation. It didn't. The whole church saw him duck out almost every week, and everyone usually knew why.

Most people know that my father invented the chicken sandwich, but who knew my mother invented text messaging? That's what it felt like, anyway, watching her notes fly down the pew and back every Sunday—iMessage, circa 1959.

CHAPTER 7

Mrs. Cathy's Girls

*M*om and Dad loved teaching our church's eighth-grade boys' and girls' Sunday School classes and did so for thirty years. They absolutely loved spending that time with brand-new teenagers in that crucial time of life. The students loved them too. Even when my parents were in their eighties, long after they had stopped teaching, they still somehow developed a strong connection with these freshly minted teenagers. It was pretty special to watch.

Mom had an especially close relationship with the girls in her class. She literally taught an entire generation of young ladies at our church, each one growing up into fine Christian women with families, ministries, careers, goals, and accomplishments of their own. Wherever these women are today, I know each one has my mother's fingerprints all over her. I've talked to so many people who not only sat through Mom's class, but who also became a part of our family. Our home was always filled to the gills every weekend with teenagers. As my parents built out our farm, they were always careful to include plenty of fun things for teens to do. We had horses, trail bikes, and four-wheelers to ride, plus all sorts of other wild outdoor adventures. Later on, Dad even built a large collection of cool antique cars to check out. Mom and Dad loved creating a safe place for students to gather, and it wasn't just for me, Dan, Bubba, and our friends; there were students milling around long after we had grown up and moved out. In fact, they still hosted these teenage boys and girls after I had children of my own. I remember several times when Mom or Dad called and asked if my children could spend the weekend at the farm to play with the students who were staying there.

My friend Julie Cook recently talked to me about what it was like growing up as one of "Mrs. Cathy's girls." That's what people in the church called Mom's class members. Julie teared up a few times while talking about my mother. I know how she feels; it's often hard for me to talk about Mom without feeling her absence now that she's gone. Still, we had a great time catching up and talking about this woman who meant so much to so many young ladies. I know what it's like to be Jeannette Cathy's daughter, of course, but I really wanted to hear how one of her students experienced her. I wanted to get a real-world, first-person look into how my mother spoke to and encouraged these girls. Julie was more than willing to share.

"I remember it like it was yesterday," Julie says. "Coming into her Sunday School class, sitting under her teaching . . . she sparked in me a love and reverence for God's Word. I didn't find out until later that she had attended seminary. As far as I knew, she was just my Sunday School teacher. But, by her very presence, she taught respect for the Word." I know exactly what Julie means. My mother radiated a reverence for Scripture. She absolutely loved absorbing the Word throughout her life. Looking back, the most enduring memory I have of my mother is seeing her at the little kitchen table in her gleaming white kitchen, crouched over her well-worn Bible and Sunday School lesson materials. I simply cannot think about my mother without seeing her hunched over a Bible. And, when she wasn't pouring Scripture *into* herself, she was pouring it *out* to others. God's Word flowed freely in her speech. It was as though a lifetime of Bible study drenched every word she spoke in the joy and power of God's Word. I love knowing that the girls in her class got to see that just as clearly as I did.

"I was never late for her Sunday School class, and I always prepared ahead of time earlier in the week," Julie continues. "I don't think I ever had a teacher that got that level of commitment from me. No one had ever expected that much out of me before. But Mrs. Cathy didn't treat us like children; she treated us like the young ladies we were becoming. She had high expectations for us, and she made us want to grow to meet them.

"There was such a tenderness in her walk with God," she recalls. "You know, in the corporate world and even in the church world, we hear a lot about raising up leaders. That's great, and the world needs godly leaders, but that wasn't Mrs. Cathy's calling. She was more concerned about raising up a generation of godly *servants*. She was very intentional about teaching us how to serve other people, how to love, and how to give of ourselves. I mean, how many leadership conferences do you hear about all the time? But when was the last time you got an email about a servanthood conference? That's where Mrs. Cathy would shine.

"There she was. She was married to Truett Cathy and they were building a huge, successful company. She could have spent her time anywhere, doing anything she wanted. She could have spent every weekend at a big country club if she wanted to! But that wasn't her. Instead, she chose to meet weekly with a group of eighth-grade girls and she went out of her way to keep up with what each one of us was doing, what was going on in our lives, and how we were growing in the Lord long after we left her class. She didn't have time for the country club; she was too busy investing in the next generation of young women."

Julie and Mom developed a special connection over their shared love of music. Mom was an incredibly gifted musician—something she passed down to her children and grandchildren. So when she saw that same passion for music in one of her Sunday School girls, she went out of her way to fan those flames. When Julie's favorite Christian artist, Evie, came through town one year, Mom bought two tickets and took Julie out for a special girls' night, just the two of them. "It was so neat to have a Sunday School teacher who took that kind of personal interest in me," Julie says. "She just wanted me to get a glimpse of what a life in Christian music might look like and to see what other musicians can do with the gifts God has given them. It's been thirty years since then, but I still think of that night every time I get on stage somewhere to sing. I've served the Lord through music for most of my life, and that's partly because Mrs. Cathy saw something in me that she wanted to encourage. That's such an incredible gift."

Mom did more than help Julie dream big; she also gave her a safe place to focus on while singing as a young girl. "Whenever I'd sing in church as a teenager, there were a couple of friendly faces I'd try to find in the crowd. Mrs. Cathy was the main one. She became an anchor for me. I'd find her sweet smile in the congregation and then I'd breathe a little easier. I'd think, *There's Mrs. Cathy. She's with me. She's for me. I'm going to make it through this song just fine.* And I did."

One Sunday morning in particular, Julie arrived to Mom's class in a huff. She'd had a rough morning and, when she finally made it to church, she realized she had a run in her pantyhose. "This was back in the day when girls and ladies wore hose to church," she jokes. "And it was a total tragedy for any girl—especially a thirteen-year-old girl—to have a run in her hose. It was my only pair, and I was stuck at church all morning with this big rip down my leg. This may seem silly now, but it was a huge deal to me in the moment. I was so upset, but I was trying to keep it together during Mrs. Cathy's Bible study. She could tell something was wrong, though. I'm not sure how, but she knew something wasn't right with me. So, she actually stopped in the middle of her lesson and said, 'Julie, are you okay, honey? What's wrong?'

"All the tension from the morning poured out of me. I said, 'Oh, Mrs. Cathy. Everything's gone wrong today, and now I have this giant run in my pantyhose. Several people have already pointed it out to me today, and I'm just so embarrassed. I just want to go home and hide for the rest of the day!'

"A lot of teachers would have blown me off or told me it was no big deal, but I'll never forget what Mrs. Cathy did. She stopped her lesson and used this opportunity to teach the whole class of girls an important lesson about grace under fire. She said, 'Girls, if that ever happens, just smile, tell the person you didn't realize you had a run, and thank them for telling you. That's it. You can choose whether or not to make it a big deal, so try to choose not to.'

"I know that doesn't sound like a life-changing moment, especially telling this story as an adult now. But back then, it was revolutionary. Teenage girls can be so terrified of someone pointing out their flaws, but Mrs. Cathy taught us a simple, straightforward trick for diffusing criticism. I've applied that to all kinds of scenarios throughout my life. It's a constant reminder to keep my head, choose my reaction, and respond to criticism with grace and a smile. It was a profound teaching moment right when I needed it the most, and I only got it because she cared enough to stop what she was doing and use that opportunity—*every* opportunity—to serve her girls."

Mom's influence has endured in Julie's life in other ways, as well. For example, Julie sought out Mom's advice when she and her future husband started talking about marriage. Many, many other women did the same. Mom often talked to her girls about how and why to make wise relationship decisions. She counseled them as they got older and started dating, and many of them, like Julie, felt like they needed "Mrs. Cathy's" stamp of approval before they said *yes* to an engagement proposal. That's a powerful legacy, knowing that Mom impacted not only these ladies' lives but their husbands and whole families, as well.

Julie honors my mother in another unique way too: with her perfume selection. "Mrs. Cathy wore one and only one perfume the entire time I knew her: Tea Rose. Tea Rose smells like you fell into a bucket of rose petals, and Mrs. Cathy wore it every Sunday. That meant our little Sunday School classroom was filled with the smell of roses. Somehow, that scent became tied in my mind to the Bible. It represents the very aroma of Christ to me, because that's exactly what Mrs. Cathy did—she exuded the aroma of Christ. Even now, I can't smell Tea Rose without thinking of Mrs. Cathy and the Word of God. In a way, I guess, heaven smells like Tea Rose to me! That's why, all the years later, the only perfume on my counter is Tea Rose. I wear it because that's what *she* wore. It makes me feel closer to her and closer to the Lord at the same time."

My mother loved Julie deeply. Their closeness represented every young lady my mother impacted over her long, rich life of service.

That's one reason why we asked Julie to sing at Mom's ninetieth birthday party and then again at her homegoing service a few years later. We wanted to be sure Julie had one last opportunity to see Mom's smiling face in the crowd, cheering her on to new heights. Fighting back tears of gratitude and love, Julie put a beautiful crown on both of these key celebrations. Her music, not to mention her sincere love for my mother, is a gift our family will never forget.

CHAPTER 8

A Priceless Penny

"Mom, you can't be serious! This is crazy! It's just a penny!" I screamed. Then I cried and stomped my feet. Then I bargained for other options. But my mother wouldn't budge. It was time for me to face the music . . . so to speak.

I was about ten years old, and it was the day of my weekly piano lesson at the home of my teacher, Mr. Edwards. My brother Dan and I had back-to-back lessons every week, so Mom sat in the car with Dan while I had my lesson, then Dan would go in while I'd wait in the car with Mom. Looking back on it now, I realize how special that weekly one-on-one time with her was for me. Sometimes we talked, but more often than not I sat there as quietly as I could while she studied her Sunday School materials and prepared to teach that week's class.

This particular day, while we were waiting on Dan to finish his lesson, Mom was working on her Bible study and I was fidgeting beside her in the front seat. I had a penny in my hand, and I kept dragging it across the dashboard, flipping it in the air, and rolling it between my fingers. After ten minutes or so, Mom finally raised her eyes over the top of her Sunday School materials and said, "Trudy, what on earth are you playing with?"

"It's just a penny," I replied.

"Where did you get it?" she asked.

That's when I realized there may be a problem. My mind flashed back to about fifteen minutes earlier, right after I had finished my piano lesson and was walking out of Mr. Edward's house. I had my piano books stuffed under one arm, and the other hand was free to explore every square inch of tabletops, framed pictures, coasters, knickknacks, and décor that stood between me and the door. I dragged my little fingers across every surface on my way out—something I've seen my own children and grandchildren do around that same age. I suppose the ten-year-old mind is anxious to explore every possible adventure that's hiding behind every surface. This day, my eyes latched onto a lone penny sitting on Mr. Edwards' coffee table. Without thinking or even slowing down, I bent over and snatched it up as I made my way to the door. It immediately felt at home in my hand, and it gave me *something* to focus my adolescent boredom on during the interminable thirty-minute wait I'd have in the car while Mom and I waited on Dan.

"Trudy," Mom repeated. "Where did you get the penny?"

Not thinking it was a big deal, I replied, "From Mr. Edwards' house. I picked it up off his coffee table." Judging by my mother's reaction, this whole penny situation was a much bigger deal than I could have imagined.

Her eyebrows shot up and she gave me a look that said, "Get comfortable, child. We're going to be here a while." She proceeded to give me one of the most memorable lectures of my life. She said, "Trudy, that's stealing, plain and simple. It may be 'just a penny' to you, but we do not take things that do not belong to us. It doesn't matter what it is or how much it's worth; it wasn't yours, and you should not have taken it." That's when she hit me with the most devastating news a young child can hear: "When Dan's lesson is over, you are going to take that penny back to Mr. Edwards, admit what you did, and apologize to him for stealing."

I was shocked and pitched one of the biggest fits of my life. I raised my voice, cried, and protested, "But it's just a penny! This is crazy! Please don't make me do this!" I didn't care about the money; I was mortified at the thought of walking back through those doors and having that embarrassing conversation with Mr. Edwards.

Mom batted down every objection. Finally, in a tone I knew meant the conversation was over, she said, "You've got about ten minutes before Dan is finished with his lesson. Use that time to figure out what you're going to say. I know you don't want to do this, but we are not leaving here until you go back in and apologize. We'll sit in this driveway all night if we have to."

That was the longest, most gut-wrenching ten minutes of my young life. I felt sick to my stomach and my breathing became fast and shallow. When I saw Dan come out through Mr. Edwards' side door, my heart sank. I poured myself out of the car, unsure if my legs would hold me up. Sadly, they did. Step by step, I made my way along the sidewalk and up the steps to the door. I looked over my shoulder to see my mother watching my every move. Mr. Edwards opened the door and said, "Hi, Trudy. Did you forget something?"

With every ounce of courage I could muster, I said, "Um, Mr. Edwards, I need to apologize to you. When I was walking out earlier, I saw a penny on your coffee table . . . and I took it. Here it is. I'm sorry for stealing from you."

My piano teacher, no doubt aware that my mother had put me up to this shocking confession, took the news pretty well. He gave me a little smirk and said, "Oh, okay. Thanks." I sulked back down the sidewalk to the car, climbed in the backseat, and sentenced my mother to several hours of the only payback I could give: the silent treatment. I pouted and whimpered, forever wounded by the pain of my humiliation.

I say that jokingly, of course, but I suppose this incident really did leave a lasting scar on me. From that day on, even up to today, I think of that experience every time I see a coin laying abandoned on the ground. From age ten, I've never once picked up a coin or random dollar I've found in a parking lot. Whenever I see one—even now in my sixties—I can't help but hear my mother's words echoing in my head, "We do not take things that do not belong to us. It doesn't matter what it is or how much it's worth." Years after this incident, after I became a mother myself, my children would get so excited to find a quarter laying unattended. Several times, I remember them saying, "Hey look! A quarter!" as they ran to pick it up. I stopped them every time. Something deep within me simply could not let them have it. It wasn't there's, even if it *was* "just a penny" or "just a quarter."

I think back to that encounter in Mr. Edwards's driveway often, and every one of my children and grandchildren has heard the story a few times. That's what made a more recent experience with my grandchildren so impactful to me and to them. John and I took a couple of our grandchildren to a baseball game. We were making our way through the old Atlanta Braves baseball stadium when I looked down and saw two $100 bills. I had never seen so much money laying on the ground before, and this ran smack into my hardline stance on not picking up money that's not mine. My grandchildren, of course, weren't so reserved about it. They screamed, "Mimi! It's two hundred bucks! Can we keep it? Please??"

The voice of my mother answered back, "No, no. It's not ours, and we do not take things that don't belong to us. It doesn't matter what it is or how much it's worth." Besides, two hundred dollars is a large sum of money. Somewhere in the park, someone was no doubt turning out their pockets or emptying their purse in a desperate search for their lost money. Even though we were not going to keep it, I did feel a certain responsibility for it. I picked it up so no one else would take it, and John and I discussed what to do. We looked around and were thrilled to see the stadium's Chick-fil-A location just a few feet away from where we found the money. What luck! If we know one thing, it's that Chick-fil-A employees are some of the best and most trustworthy people around. So, John walked over and spoke to the team members behind the counter. He told them we had some money and gave them his cell number. He said, "We'll be in our seats throughout the game, and I've got the money in my pocket. If anyone happens to come by here saying they lost any money, call me on my cell. I'll walk back over here and give it to its rightful owner."

With that, we struck out to find our seats and enjoy the game. Throughout the game, though, our grandchildren kept asking about the money. "Do you still have it, Papa? Will we be able to keep it if no one calls? What could we do with it?" I used that opportunity to tell them once again about what my mother taught me about taking things that don't belong to us. I told them all about how hard it was for me to go back to Mr. Edwards and admit what I had done. I explained that I'd never been able to pick up even a loose penny in a parking lot after that because I always heard my mother's voice ringing in my ears. And John and I were careful to explain to them exactly what we had told the Chick-fil-A employees and why it was so important to be honest and trustworthy, even when (or *especially* when) no one else is looking. It may not have been as steeped in drama as my own penny-stealing lesson was at their age, but I think they got the message nonetheless. I like to think my mother would have been proud.

Fortunately, about halfway through the game, John got a call on his cellphone from the stadium Chick-fil-A. A young mom had accidentally dropped the money on her way to the bathroom, and she had been running to every nearby kiosk and food vender in a panic asking if anyone had turned it in. John walked back to the store, met the young woman, and gladly gave the money back. She was so relieved! She told John she hadn't even returned to her seat since losing the money, because she knew her husband would be so upset with her.

This was a powerful moment for me, because it gave me an up-close look at what my mother was trying to teach me more than fifty years earlier. If we had kept that two hundred dollars, we could have used it to buy a gameday souvenir for our grandchildren. They would have thought it was their lucky day. That young woman, however, would not have felt so fortunate. That money could have represented her entire grocery budget for the month. She might have needed it to buy clothes for her children. Or, maybe she had saved up for a couple of months to earn enough money to take her family out to a ballgame for a special treat. Who knows? That money could have meant *everything* to her in that moment, and we could have ruined her week by keeping what belonged to her. We could have sent her home in tears without ever knowing (or caring) who she was—but my mother would not allow it. Even though this was a few years after Mom's passing, her legacy lived on, protecting a stranger's money and giving her great-grandchildren a lesson I hope they never forget. I know I never will.

It may have been *just a penny*, but the lesson Mom taught me that day was priceless.

CHAPTER 9

Music, the Language of Our Family

*O*ur days on the farm were filled with music. In many ways, it was the very *language* of our family. There were practically no days that didn't involve some form of musical interaction, and that was 100 percent due to my mother's undeniable musical genius. Even from a young age, she could pick up just about any instrument and figure out how to play something beautiful. She was singing and dancing on stages throughout Atlanta from the age of three, winning awards nearly every time she appeared before a crowd. As we've already seen, she even spent an entire summer as a young girl traveling to a number of churches as the featured musical guest for week-long revivals. In college, she played the trumpet—a surprisingly difficult instrument to learn—for the Georgia State Girls Military Band, helping them win many national band competitions. Whether it was performing on stage, singing in front of a crowd, playing the piano at church and at home, serving in the church choir, belting out gospel songs on her trumpet, or singing sweetly to her heavenly Father as she did housework, music flowed freely out of my mother. It was part of her spirit; you couldn't help but *feel* the music in her whenever she was around.

This meant her children had no choice about whether or not they were going to play an instrument. It was never even a question. I remember my mother plopping me down on the piano bench long before my feet could even reach the pedals. She did the same with my brothers. Music may not have been a big deal in my dad's family (he wasn't musically gifted *at all*), but it was important for the McNeils. And, since the three of us were half-McNeil, we had to speak the language of music.

Dan can still vividly remember his first trumpet at age ten. Our school's music teacher, Mr. Woods, was encouraging all the boys and girls to find an instrument that really *spoke* to them. He led several meetings with parents and students to not only help the children develop a love for music but to also get the parents involved. This was right up my mother's alley. She gave Dan the freedom to explore the options on his own, of course, because she wanted his instrument to be a very personal expression for him. You can imagine how thrilled she was when he came home from one of those meetings with a trumpet—an instrument she'd played as a child and young woman.

Dan says, "I remember opening it up when I got it home. It was an Olds brand trumpet, and I thought, *This is* my *trumpet*. I'll never forget the smell of that old velvet mixed with alcohol that hit me in the face whenever I opened the case. And my mother taught me how to play it."

Mom also sent Dan to expert teachers to better hone his craft. "She was really incredible about getting all of us to our different lessons," he says. "She arranged for me to take lessons from John Head, one of the most celebrated trumpeters in Atlanta with the Atlanta Symphony Orchestra. She'd drive me thirty-five minutes to get there, sit outside in the car for an hour during my lesson, and then drive us another thirty-five minutes home. And then she'd drive me all over town to listen to my teacher perform because he was so good. She didn't just want me to learn *how* to play it; she wanted me to learn *why* to play it. She wanted me to develop not just the skills but the *love* of music. And it worked. Now, more than fifty years later, I still practice my horn at six in the morning before coming into work most days."

When Dan shared this with me, what I found most interesting is how he says playing music affected his life as a leader. Today, he's the CEO of Chick-fil-A. He's the leader of a multibillion-dollar company, and the love of music he learned from our mother is such a perfect counterpoint to the love of business and customer service he learned from our dad. He says, "The love of the arts and humanities, the love of education, the idea of developing yourself and growing yourself . . . it's all in the DNA the three of us got from her. I still have those passions today. They're very much woven into my life and they've greatly affected my leadership role at Chick-fil-A."

"Music not only nurtures my soul," he continues, "it's also given me a wonderful way of personal expression. It's helped me as a leader to trust the *feelings* side of my heart and express it in an effective way."

I couldn't agree more. However, those lessons weren't always easily learned—for Mom or for us. She had three children playing different instruments, and she had to run us all around town for our various lessons every week. Dan and I took piano, Dan had his trumpet lessons, Bubba had trombone lessons, I had clarinet lessons; I can't imagine how many miles Mom drove—not to mention the hours she spent in the car—all for the love of music. And then there was the practice. Oh, the practice! All three of us had to put in at least thirty minutes a day of productive practice, either first thing in the morning or right after we got up from the dinner table. We had little cards from our music teachers that we had to fill out showing what we played, how long we played, how often we played, and so on. We'd practice, fill out our cards, and then get Mom to sign off on them. She was our co-teacher, supporter, manager, personal driver, and biggest fan all rolled into one!

She was also a great bandmate and accompanist for us. Mom would join Dan, Bubba, and me in the little farmhouse living room to play beautiful family concerts throughout the day and nearly every weekend. She'd be at the piano while Dan played his trumpet, Bubba played his trombone, and I joined in on the clarinet. Dad got jealous of all our musical ability every now and then—a talent he sorely lacked. In fact, he snuck out to the music store one weekend and came back home with his very own violin. My mother greeted him at the door and said, "Truett, what are you doing with that?"

"I'm going to learn how to play it!" he replied proudly.

"Well, okay," she said with an air of doubt in her voice. "But why'd you pick the violin?"

"I was looking at all the instruments and saw that this one only had four strings instead of six. I figured that'd make it easier to learn!"

Mom held back a laugh at his reasoning. However, just as he said, Dad signed up for violin lessons the next week at the Band

Box in East Point, just down the street from the Dwarf House. When he came back home from his first lesson, Mom asked, "How'd it go?"

"Great!" he said. "I learned two songs. The teacher said he's going out of town next week, so he'll call me to schedule my next lesson when he gets back." That call never came; his teacher dumped him! Apparently, Dad's natural skills as a businessman and restaurateur did not translate to the musical realm, so my poor father only ever learned how to scratch out "Mary Had a Little Lamb." He was exaggerating a bit when he said he learned how to play *two* songs. The other song he said he knew was "Merrily We Roll Along," which is the exact same tune as "Mary Had a Little Lamb!" Sometimes, the dogs on the farm would "sing" along with him when he tried to play. My mother, however, kept his violin and mastered it pretty quickly . . . much to Dad's chagrin.

Soon after, my mother felt bad that my dad felt so left out by our family music sessions, so she bought him a set of high-hat cymbals. She figured all he'd have to do is sit on the sofa and tap his foot to the beat of our tunes, and he'd be able to be our family's percussionist. He was excited to give it a try, but it didn't go as well as Mom had hoped. Dad could never find the right tempo, so he threw the rest of us off beat every time he tried. Mom's patience dwindled until one day the cymbals disappeared from our living room, never to be seen again.

There was one family musical act that my brothers and I *didn't* always enjoy. That was performing at the Dwarf House. Mom had what she thought was a great idea when the three of us were young: she'd dress us up in costumes reminiscent of the dwarves from *Snow White* and have us sing for the lunch and dinner crowds at Dad's restaurant. She was so excited about the idea that she could hardly stand it. She recruited our Granny—a longtime professional costumer—to make our costumes, and a friend wrote the lyrics for her. I will never forget the experience of standing between my brothers in my silly silk dwarf costume singing that Dwarf House song to the tune of "Hey, Look Me Over."

Hey! Take the family out for a treat.
Bring them to the Dwarf House for the best to eat.
The most modern building, finest homemade pies,
Delicious steak plates served with salad and French fries.

Dwarf burgers are the best served anywhere, folks.
Made from the choicest US grade meat.
Our service, too, is friendly
And just cannot be beat.
Smiley Dwarf is here to greet you wherever you may look,
So, folks, don't stay home and cook!

We have a dwarf mural moving on the wall,
Thick shakes in flavors that are the best of all.
So, whether your name is Smith or even if it's Jones,
We know you'll love our chicken, folks, because it has
no bones.

And we'll be mighty pleased friends,
Yes, we'll think it's fine,
To have you come and see our patio and dine.
So, come out and treat the family for a feast fit for a king.
Dwarf serves you the best of everything!

Come to the Dwarf House . . . and eat!

No, it never made the Top 40, but it was fun for the regulars at the restaurant to see us perform. Dad had built great relationships with his customers, and they appreciated seeing his wife and children running around doing *our part* for the business.

My days on Dwarf duty aren't quite over yet. Today, many Chick-fil-A locations have history boards with old photographs of the early days of Chick-fil-A and the Dwarf House. There, proudly displayed on these boards, you can often find a picture of my brothers and me in our full Dwarf regalia belting out our tune into a microphone. What you *can't* see in that photo, though, is our mother laughing and singing along in the crowd. She loved to see us perform. It was a funny sight, sure, but I think it was more about seeing her children enjoy music.

That became such a special memory for all of us that Dan, Bubba, and I recreated it as part of her big ninetieth birthday party celebration. There, in front of more than a hundred guests, the three of us took the stage and shared a single microphone to perform her famous (or maybe *infamous*) Dwarf song. We didn't quite look the same. I had a few more wrinkles and my brothers had a lot less hair than we did fifty years earlier, but that didn't stop us from honoring her in this special way. Our dwarf costumes no longer fit, but the love and pride we felt singing for her still did.

The rest of the family didn't escape the songs that day either. One of Mom's most precious moments was the sight of her three children and twelve grandchildren with our spouses completely filling the stage as we sang "The Instrument Song" for her. It was such a silly moment, with more than twenty people crammed in shoulder to shoulder singing rounds and imitating the sounds of clarinets, violins, trumpets, horns, and drums. I don't think Mom thought it was silly, though. She was sitting right in front of the large crowd, just a few feet from the stage. Her beautiful face was beaming with a smile that stretched ear to ear as she mouthed the words along with us. Of all the gifts we gave her over a lifetime of birthdays, I believe that meant the most to her: the sight of her children and grandchildren rejoicing in the gift of music she had given each of us, giving her back just a sliver of the music she'd put in all our hearts.

CHAPTER 10

Misadventures in Marriage

"Cathy ladies must be like swans: calm and peaceful on the surface, but below, you're paddling your legs off just to stay afloat in all this craziness!" I heard my mother say that about a million times throughout my life. It's a lesson she shared with my sisters-in-law, Rhonda and Cindy, when my brothers got married. It's something she was sure to tell each of her granddaughters *and* each of her grandsons' new wives when they walked down the aisle. Every woman in the Cathy family and extended family has gotten the message loud and clear: being part of this family is an adventure!

I'm sure that's a hard-fought lesson my mother learned throughout her sixty-five-year marriage to my father. For example, there was their infamous trip to Savannah, Georgia, in 1964. President Lyndon B. Johnson was running for reelection, and his wife, Lady Bird Johnson, was on a whistle-stop train tour of the South as part of the campaign. Her tour took her through Savannah, which is only a four-hour drive from Atlanta. My parents thought it would be fun to drive down there for a little getaway to see the First Lady's tour and even bring her a sample of Dad's new invention, the Chick-fil-A sandwich. He'd only been serving it in the Dwarf House for a short time, and this was three years before he opened the first Chick-fil-A mall location, so it was just a local treat at the time. He thought, *How great would it be to treat the First Lady with a Chick-fil-A sandwich?*

My Granny came to stay on the farm with my brothers and me while they were gone, and two important things happened in our family while they were gone that week. First, a beautiful, red-headed Amazon parrot appeared out of nowhere on some bushes in our back yard. Granny managed to catch it, and from then on, Polly the Parrot was a part of our family. I'll tell you more about Polly in the next chapter, because there's a lot to say about her!

Second, my brothers and I bought Dad a motorcycle. His interest in motorcycles had been growing for years but he hadn't gotten one yet. He started by getting into minibikes and then scooters. He'd ride them whenever he got the chance, and he kept talking about getting a motorcycle for himself, but something always got in the way. That was just fine with my mother. She was nervous enough about all of us riding horses so often, especially after she broke her leg riding once. One fall was all it took for her to give up riding for good, even though we had all that farmland and plenty of horses. If seeing her husband gallop around on a horse made her wince, you can only imagine how she felt about him tearing across the property on a high-powered motorcycle!

Anyway, we somehow managed to buy him a motorcycle (with his own money), and Dan, Bubba, Granny, and I couldn't wait for them to get home to see it. You'd think we'd have put it in the garage or under the carport, right? Wrong. A present like this deserved a bigger spectacle! So, we parked it right in the center of our living room in front of the fireplace. Santa Claus couldn't have done a better job with the presentation than the four of us did.

I should probably take a moment, though, to tell you about my mother's housekeeping at this time. She kept the house in pristine condition at all times. The white carpet was perfectly clean and vacuumed, the sofa was positioned *just so*, the throw pillows were exactly in the right spot. Plus, she had just started getting into the color white, so sparkling new white accent pieces had begun popping up here and there. I have no idea how she kept it so clean with all of us coming in and out from the muddy fields all the time, but she did. Outside may have been a farm, but inside was a showroom. Of course, this particular week, we'd turned it into a motorcycle showroom.

On the day my parents were scheduled to come home, we all anxiously watched for Mom and Dad's car coming up the driveway. Finally, after what seemed like an eternity, we heard the car approaching the house. Mom and Dad came in through the back door into the kitchen, where we greeted them with huge smiles and giggles. After the obligatory hugs and kisses, we ushered Dad into the living room where his treasure awaited. When he rounded the corner and saw the motorcycle sitting in the living room, the most spectacular smile spread across his face. He started laughing and immediately ran over to inspect his new toy.

Mother, on the other hand, reacted a bit differently. She asked all the questions you'd expect: "Where did you get this?" "How did you pay for it?" And, most importantly, "What is this thing doing in my living room?" She was halfway across the room when Dad did the unthinkable. In his excitement, Dad sat down on the bike, set the key in the starting position, and then cranked it—right there in the immaculately clean living room. A cloud of dark black smoke shot out of the bike's exhaust and engine fumes immediately filled the house. Dad was laughing his head off as he continually revved the engine. Dan, Bubba, and I were cheering him on. But Mom . . . Mom was reaching for the broom. She came at him swinging her broom like Babe Ruth. She bopped him on the head to get his attention and yelled, "The living room is no place for a motorcycle!" as she whacked him on the back a few times to drive the point home. Now under pressure and not sure what to do, Dad did the only thing he could think of: he put the bike in gear and drove it across the living room and out the front door with three children roaring with laughter, an angry wife turning a bright shade of red, and a befuddled mother-in-law trailing behind him. We spent the rest of the day outside playing with Dad and his new bike while Mom wiped, mopped, vacuumed, and scrubbed the ghost of the motorcycle off every surface of her picture-perfect living room.

The Great Motorcycle Incident of '64 wasn't the only time my father's enthusiasm nearly brought the house down. More than forty years later, when my parents were in their eighties, the guys who helped on the farm came in to find evidence of a late-night housefire—and my father sitting at the kitchen table with his head in his hands. Chris Phillips, who's helped on the property for many years, saw a pile of burnt towels under the carport as he came in that morning. He walked through the back door and saw Dad alone at the table. Chris told me later, "I could tell pretty quickly that Truett had been through the wringer." He also noticed the smell of smoke and burnt wood throughout the house, so he said, "Truett, what in the world happened here? Are you guys okay?"

That's when Mom burst through the door into the kitchen. "Oh, Chris. Let me tell you what he did. You're not going to believe it." Mom and Dad had friends over for dinner the night before, which wasn't unusual at all. However, Mom had put out a new centerpiece for the night on their long dining room table. Dad also thought it'd be nice to have candles on the table to really create a special atmosphere as they entertained their guests. The night went great, everyone had a good time, and their friends left around ten o'clock. Mom and Dad were cleaning up and chatting afterward when they began to smell smoke. They ran back into the dining room to find a raging inferno sitting atop their beautiful dining room table! Dad had apparently left a candle burning a little too close to Mom's new centerpiece, and the whole thing had gone up in flames.

Despite his age at the time, Dad was still in pretty good health and immediately jumped into action. Of course, the crew that worked the property had installed fire extinguishers all through the house by then, but Dad's early 1920's upbringing took over. Rather than reaching for the nearest fire extinguisher, he ran through the house to the bathroom and grabbed an armful of towels. He knew the fire was still small enough to smother, but it wouldn't be long before the ceiling and wall caught fire. He had to act fast!

Mom saw him running back from the bathroom and yelled, "What are you doing with my good towels?"

"I've got to put this fire out!" he answered.

"Not with my good towels, you aren't!" she shot back at him.

So there they were, bickering about which towels were too nice to use to save the house from burning down while a giant fire spread across their dining room table. Mom told him which towels she'd be willing to part with and sent him off on a second trip to the bathroom. Exasperated, he ran back through with a new armload of towels. He shot a look at her as her darted past and asked, "*These?!*"

"Yes, *those!*" she replied.

With her blessing, he sacrificed her not-nearly-as-good towels on the Altar of the Burning Centerpiece. By the time he had the fire out, they realized the ceiling had been scorched and was probably about one minute away from lighting up. At that point, it would have taken a lot more than a load of linens to put the fire out—no matter how nice the towels were.

Dad got an earful about towels, centerpieces, candles, and fire safety that night and into the next morning when Chris found him hunched over the kitchen table. I don't think he'd ever in his life been so glad to leave for work as he was that morning . . . even though a faint cloud of smoke and regret clung to his suit as he left.

There are so many stories like that in our family. When Mom said "I do" on September 19, 1948, she had no idea what the future held for them. She could not have imagined what all she was saying *I do* to. It wasn't always easy, and it wasn't always fun. They fussed and fought sometimes. She missed him terribly during his long work days. She struggled to figure out how to get by on a big farm with three young children and no one else to count on. She got a little frustrated when he brought home unexpected dinner guests at the last minute—or when he missed dinner altogether. Or when he set the table on fire. Or when he started his motorcycle in her living room. But she loved him. She loved him more and more every day until the day he died—and probably even more after that. She never let the little annoyances of married life distract her from the joy of living every day to the fullest with her true love. My brother Dan says, "That's the definition of a perfect marriage, when two imperfect people make a commitment to do whatever it takes to hang in there with each other. And that's just what they did."

CHAPTER 11

Animal House

Growing up surrounded by animals was perfectly natural to us as children; it's all we knew from a young age. For my mother, though, all this was still very new. She grew up in the city and suburbs of Atlanta and, as far as I know, never even had as much as a house cat or dog as a child. She remained pet-free during her years at college and seminary, and she and Dad didn't get a pet when they married and moved into the little house he and Uncle Horace built near the Dwarf Grill. To go from that relatively animal-free existence to life on a crazy farm was a bit of a culture shock for her. To be honest, we didn't make it easy for her to get used to, but she still did her best to turn these moments into special memories.

We adopted one of our favorite pets in 1964. Actually, I guess you could say *she* adopted *us*. It happened when my parents took their trip to Savannah to see Lady Bird Johnson on her whistle-stop train tour and Granny was staying with us on the farm. One afternoon while they were gone, my Granny, brothers, and I were all sitting in the kitchen playing and talking. We looked out the window and saw the most amazing sight: a gorgeous parrot with a bright red head perched on some bushes outside. Granny told us to run and grab a big towel as she crept out the door. The parrot watched her approach but didn't seem that bothered by her. In one sweeping motion, Granny threw a towel over the beautiful bird and bundled it up so it couldn't get away. We brought it inside, found something to put it in, and checked it for any evidence of where it came from. After all, I'm not aware of any normal migration patterns that would call for Amazon parrots to fly through North Georgia farmlands. Her wings had not been clipped, though, which indicated she probably hadn't been kept as a pet before. To this day, we have no idea where she came from.

Granny, whose grandparents had kept parrots long before, was thrilled. My brothers and I were *even more* excited. We named her Polly (of course), got a cage for her, and couldn't wait for Mom and Dad to get home to meet her. Of course, you'll remember Polly's welcome to the family was slightly interrupted by the motorcycle that was also waiting on Dad in the living room. After Mom shooed Dad (and his running motorcycle) out of the house, she was able to meet Polly. The two hit it off from the start, and Polly became a part of our family for the next thirty years. That's right—thirty years! I had no idea parrots lived so long! If I had, maybe we would have thought twice about forcing that kind of lifelong commitment on my mother.

Over the next few years, Mom spent time teaching Polly how to talk. And, much to my delight and constant annoyance, one of her first words was "Trudy." I can't tell you how many times I'd be studying, playing the piano, or sitting in my room when I heard a sweet voice call out, "Truuuuudy!" I'd come running to my mother saying, "I'm right here, Mom. What do you need?" But, of course, it wasn't my mother calling me. It was that bird. She somehow called my name in the exact same voice and tone as my mother. Mom laughed every time it happened. It was her own little practical joke, one of the few ways she had to get back at me for all the mischief I caused as a child.

Mom also taught Polly a phrase that never failed to get a laugh out of our family and any guests we had at the farm—especially people who worked for my dad. We'd be in the middle of dinner or chatting in the kitchen when Polly's favorite cheer suddenly filled the house: "Mm! Mm! Chick-fil-A!" She was probably our greatest spokesman in those early days!

Believe it or not, a mysterious Amazon parrot wasn't the most exotic animal Mom ever had to put up with inside the house. The most unusual farm animal we ever had was our little friend Pee Wee—a South American squirrel monkey. That's right, Mom kept a *monkey* in the house for a while. Neither my brothers nor I remember where, when, or how Pee Wee came to live with us. You'd think that's the kind of memory that would stay locked in our brains forever, but apparently it wasn't significant enough for us to remember. By that point, he was just one of many animals that lived with us on that sprawling dreamland.

Mom kept Pee Wee in a large cage in our basement, and we even had a little leash for him so he could join us outside. He had the sweetest little face, with his dark eyes sitting in a field of white through the middle of his face. He looked like a tiny bandit wearing a white mask. Just Google "squirrel monkey" and you'll see what I mean. We sure loved that little guy . . . but he didn't last very long. Tragedy struck on the farm one day when Pee Wee came face to face with a coyote. Let's just say the coyote won.

As much as we loved Pee Wee and Polly, the hands-down best pets we ever got were a Christmas surprise. I was around six years old, and we'd been on the farm for a few years before Mom and Dad finally gave in to our biggest request: ponies! One Christmas morning when I was around six years old, my brothers and I ran to the living room to see our new toys and treasures. After unwrapping the usual assortment of Christmas gifts, Mom led us to the back door. When we stepped out, we saw a trail of streamers leading from the farmhouse door out to a small shelter a good distance away. Dan, Bubba, and I raced down the path our parents had marked and burst through the doors of the make-shift stable. There, two perfect little ponies stood side by side, just waiting to join three young children on countless farm adventures. My brothers and I shrieked with excitement as we raced over to pet, hug, brush, and greet our new best friends whom we named Captain and Dolly.

We learned that ponies, like many animals, *imprint* on people quickly. Since Captain and Dolly were still young, they took to us almost immediately. They knew they were *our* ponies. So, even when we weren't riding them, the pair had a tendency of following us around the property like a dog might do. They were always trailing behind us, ready to romp and play at a moment's notice. Once we figured out they'd follow us just about anywhere, the thought occurred to us: *Wouldn't it be funny if Captain and Dolly followed us inside the house?* We weren't sure they'd do it, but we *were* certain Mom must have had some unspoken rule against bringing ponies into the living room. It was too great of an idea to ignore, though. So, we put our theory to the test.

One afternoon while Mom was in the basement doing laundry, we opened the back door and quietly led Captain inside to the living room. We had to choke down our laughter to not ruin Mom's surprise. Much to our delight, the pony didn't hesitate; he walked right in like he owned the place. He was just as eager to play with us *inside* as he was *outside.* We led him to the fireplace, which was in perfect view of the door coming up from the basement. After posing him in front of the fireplace, we yelled, "Mom! Can you come up here for a second? We want to show you something."

We heard her start to shuffle up the stairs, heading our way. Dan, Bubba, and I took our places beside Captain and waited. When Mom came through the basement door with her arms wrapped around a full laundry basket of clean clothes, a mixture of shock and bewilderment spread across her face. I could tell it took a moment for her to fully process what she was looking at. When it finally struck her, she screamed, "What is that thing doing in my living room? Get him out! Get him out right now!"

My brothers and I broke out laughing. The idea of a pony in mom's perfectly clean white living room was the funniest thing to us at the time. Hey, at least Captain's white coat matched Mom's décor! As irritated as she was, Mom couldn't help but laugh with us. She even took a picture of the tiny horse at the fireplace before she kicked him—and the three of us—out of the house for the afternoon.

As we collected more pets, Mom found more surprises in her living room. Polly, Pee Wee, Captain, and Dolly lived in perfect harmony with our menagerie of dogs, cats, ducks, cows, horses, and pigs. Somehow, my city-born-and-bred mother took it all in stride, even when we brought most of them inside for our frequent living-room animal parades.

When Mom and Dad originally moved onto the farm, I don't think she ever expected to see a parrot and a monkey riding a pony across her living room. But it happened . . . a lot. And, to her credit, it always made her laugh.

Jeannette was born in 1922 and raised by her mother, Ida Irene McNeil. Her father left when she was just three months old.

In 1925 at the age of three, "Little Jeannette" sang and danced at the Lowes Grand Theatre in Atlanta as the youngest performer onstage.

*At just six years old, Jeannette won a silver loving cup trophy
and was crowned the best dancer in Atlanta in 1928!*

*Jeannette traveled with Truett's sister Agnes and her husband,
Rev. Dock Edwards, as their guest soloist for church revivals.*

Jeannette played trumpet for the Georgia State Girl's Military Band, winning national band competitions.

Truett's family, which included his parents, two brothers, and four sisters, lived just down the street from Jeannette.

Truett and Jeannette were married on
September 19, 1948, at West End Baptist Church.
Jeannette's wedding gown custom-made by her mother, Ida.

*Jeannette cared deeply for her mother, Ida, and celebrated
her life each year with friends and family.*

*Truett and Jeannette's home for 58 years, and the
setting of so many family stories on the farm.*

Guilty as charged! Dan, Trudy, (and Bubba) returned empty-handed from their mission to capture a dead cow's heart for show-and-tell.

Trudy, Dan, and Bubba with Polly the parrot, a family pet for 30 years.

Jeannette's children, Dan, Bubba, and Trudy, singing in their dwarf costumes for customers at the Dwarf House.

Dan, Bubba, and Trudy recreating childhood memories singing the "Dwarf House Song," as Jeannette stands to the side, proudly looking on.

*Truett, Jeannette, and their assistant,
Brooksie Kirk, at a restaurant show.*

*Jeannette and Truett enjoyed hosting friends Bill and Gloria Gaither
in their home and at the Chick-fil-A office on several occasions.*

Jeannette proudly wore her Chick-fil-A pin, a Christmas gift from Truett upon opening 17 mall locations in the 1970s.

Jeannette with her daughter, Trudy, and granddaughter Angela Fielder, celebrating the Grand Opening of Chick-fil-A Greystone (Operator Brent Fielder) and the passing of the Chick-fil-A Pin (March 2015).

Inspired by their mother's musical talent, Dan played trumpet and Bubba played trombone. They created their own band, the Chick-A-Juana Brass, and wore costumes made by Jeannette's mother.

Jeannette's musical abilities encouraged her grandchildren Joy (clarinet), John (trumpet), Angela (violin), and David White (violin).

Jeannette throws a polka-dotted, chicken pox birthday party for her granddaughter Joy (1992).

Jeannette learned about her Heavenly Father's love while attending church as a child. She is seen here at church with her grandchildren Mark and Rachel.

Jeannette shown speaking at a Christian women's retreat in 2007.

Ty Yokum receives the Jeannette Cathy Service Award, the highest award given to Chick-fil-A Support Center Staff (2016).

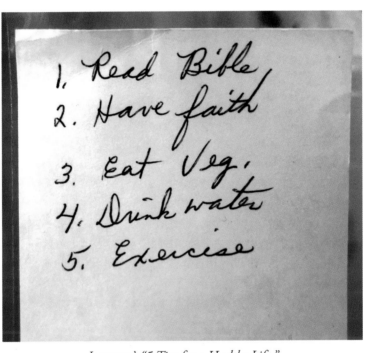

Jeannette's "5 Tips for a Healthy Life,"
found taped to her bathroom mirror.

Jeannette crammed as many pictures of her family as possible on the shelves of her home.

Three generations of Cathy family members during an annual family retreat in Florida (2009).

Jeannette was a self-taught artist. At the age of 65 she bought her first canvas and oils and completed her painting of "The Lady," an imaginative figure, not long after.

Trudy showing her grandchildren Jeannette's unfinished, half-realized portrait of Truett, found in her mother's art room after Jeannette's death.

Jeannette with great-grandson, Maverick, just days before her passing (2015).

As the only daughter, Trudy and her mother, Jeannette, shared a special bond (2010).

CHAPTER 12

A Cow Heart for Christmas

Growing up on the farm, my brothers and I pretty much had the run of the entire 262 acres. It was the most incredible playground any child could imagine. Mom gave us only one rule: we had to stay within eyeshot of the house. If we could see the house, we were in the clear; if we couldn't, we were out of bounds. It seemed like a clear, simple rule—one that'd be easy for three responsible children to follow. Of course, my brothers and I rarely did.

The 1950s and 1960s were a much different time for children than today. There were no screens to get glued to: no video games, no cellphones, no iPads, no computers. We did have a television, but we rarely turned it on. So, when we weren't in school, our days were spent either inside practicing music or outside exploring every nook and cranny of the farm. Sometimes, we even stayed within sight of the house.

Once we stepped outside, our ears were filled with the sounds of all God's creatures, great and small. We'd chase rabbits, chirp at the birds, brush our horses, and irritate the cows with our incessant mooing. Sometimes, the animals made life a dream; other times, it must have looked more like a horror movie. One Christmas in particular comes to mind. Mom had decorated the house with her typical holiday flare. The tree in the living room was a master-piece. There were other trees, wreaths, ribbons, packages, Santas, and holiday scenes all throughout the house. Our little farmhouse looked and felt like a Norman Rockwell painting all through the month of December. There was only one thing missing: a picture of three smiling children standing in front of the Christmas tree covered in blood, sweat, and mud. Fortunately for my mother, we were happy to oblige.

My brothers and I were young and especially bored during our Christmas break from school. One morning, as we were trying to think of something exciting to do, we hatched a grotesque plan. One of our cows had recently died, and Dad had disposed of it by hauling it off to the outskirts of the property. On the far edge of the farm, there was a hidden swamp area that had become his default cattle graveyard. We children weren't supposed to go there, especially since it was out of view from the house. However, the thought of a hidden, swampy cow cemetery was just too much for three young children to resist. We decided that day that we would not only travel out to the swamp, but that we'd come back with an actual cow heart. We'd be the heroes of show-and-tell when school started back!

We collected the few things we needed—Mom's large water-melon knife and a five-gallon glass pickle jar to hold the bloody treasure—and we were off. *Over the river and through the woods, to cut out a heart we go!* The farther we went, the smaller the house became in the distance until it vanished completely, meaning we were officially out of bounds and breaking the rules. No matter; we had important work to do that day . . . *for science!*

At the far edge of the property, we pushed back some brush and found the swamp. More importantly, we found the cow corpse Dad had dragged out there two days earlier. It looked different than I was expecting. It was swollen and puffed up, and flies had started buzzing around. There was also a terrible odor in the air, a horrible mixture of swamp and death. Undeterred, my brothers and I crept forward. I held the jar while Dan advanced with the knife. He raised it high above the cow and then thrust it into the belly of the beast. Now, things happened at this point that I probably shouldn't say in this book. The sight of the cow splitting open. The sound of the gasses escaping like a leaking balloon. The taste that immediately filled the back of my throat. It was all horrifying. The worst part by a mile, though, was the *smell.*

My goodness, that smell. The putrid smell of death shot out of the cow's belly and hit the three of us in the face like a freight train. It was overwhelming; I could hardly process it. Dan, Bubba, and I immediately started screaming. We tore out of there in a flash without our prize. The only thing that mattered at that point was getting home to fresh air and maybe a bath. We ran nearly the entire length of that farm faster than we'd ever run before. Mom saw us through the back window and ran out to meet us. Seeing her three children running toward the house, screaming, splattered in blood, and holding a giant knife must have been quite an experience. I'm sure it would have completely freaked out most mothers. Not ours.

We told her the whole story in vivid detail, including the part about us breaking her one rule and traveling too far into the hidden parts of the property. She looked at us for a moment—Dan drenched in cow blood holding the knife, Bubba still catching his breath and pinching his nose, and me with the empty pickle jar in my hands—and she burst out laughing. "Nothing like this ever happened when I lived in town!" she cried.

Before she cleaned us up, she wanted to commemorate the special occasion. She brought us into her spotless living room in front of her picture-perfect Christmas tree. We were still a swampy, muddy mess, so we had to be careful on the stainless white carpet. She posed Dan with his knife and me with the jar. There, in front of the Christmas tree, Mom took one of our family's favorite holiday portraits ever. We had failed to claim our intended prize, but we got something so much more valuable: an unforgettable memory, a classic family picture, and a laugh out of a mother who should have grounded us for weeks.

CHAPTER 13

The Three Ms

Throughout Mom and Dad's thirty-year Sunday School teaching career, they loved getting to know thirteen- and fourteen-year-old children, and they always felt a special closeness to young teens. The boys and girls were just coming into their own as young people, bright and full of ideas. My parents marveled at some of the things they would say and insights they'd have about the Bible and about life in general. They'd often compare notes after church on Sundays. Mom would say something like, "You won't believe what Pam said this morning!" Dad would reply, "Yeah, but let me tell you about T.J.!" They loved watching how their students' minds worked, and nothing thrilled them more than seeing a young teenager *get* the meaning of the week's Bible lesson.

Because they earned their students' trust, Mom and Dad also got to hear a lot of their complaints and frustrations. Early on in their teaching, they noticed a common theme among the children in their classes. The boys and girls were frustrated that they weren't allowed to make many big decisions for themselves. These children were riding the line between adolescence and adulthood. They yearned to be grown-ups, but they still needed the direction and boundaries offered by their parents. For these few crucial years, they were stuck in what you might call a *now-and-not-yet* state. They *wanted* to make their own decisions, but they weren't quite ready yet. So, they often grew more and more frustrated, lashing out at their parents and desperately searching for *something* they could control for themselves. This was just as true in the 1960s as it is today.

After hearing so many girls complain about not being able to make decisions for themselves, Mom started teaching her class members about "The Three Ms." This was something she and Dad came up with to give eighth graders a broader perspective on the three most important decisions they'd ever make. Every girl who came through my mother's class over her three decades of teaching heard her talk about The Three Ms several times. I know I personally heard it countless times because I got it nonstop from *both* my parents!

Mom told her Sunday School girls, "I know you're frustrated that your parents seem to make all your decisions for you. I know you think you're ready to make big decisions for yourself. But listen, if you can just wait until you're a little older, you'll be able to make the most important decisions of your life for yourself. These are the three things that will shape your entire life. These are the areas that will give you a rich, warm, successful, rewarding, happy life—or give you a sad, worrisome, stressful, empty, meaningless life. In all my years, I've found that everything comes down to these three things. And, if you pay attention now and work really hard on these three things at thirteen, I know you'll be prepared to make the right decisions when the time comes. Do you want to know what the three biggest decisions of your life are?"

Every girl in the class would be glued to Mom's face by this point. Who wouldn't want to know at thirteen what the three most important and life-changing decisions of their adult life would be? The girls felt like they were getting inside information, like my mother was giving them a peek behind the grown-up curtain that their parents kept closed.

Mom would continue, "Well, girls, it all comes down to the three most important decisions you will ever make:

1. Who is going to be *master* of your life?
2. Who will be your *mate* for life?
3. What will be your *mission* in life?

Master, Mate, and Mission. The Three Ms. If you get these three things right, girls, you can do anything and go anywhere you want in life." Let me break these things down for you the way my mother always did for me.

First, who is going to be the master of your life? Mom always said this is the most important question any of us will ever face. She stressed to her teen girls that it's a question each of us has to make for ourselves. As I've raised my own daughters now and have granddaughters approaching their teen years, I can see why Mom always stressed the importance of making this decision for yourself. Young girls often get so frustrated about the decisions they *can't* make— what to wear, where to go, who to spend time with, how long they can be out. In a season of life when independence feels like the most important thing in the world, young girls can feel more hemmed in by their parents than ever. That's why Mom always gave the girls a vision for where they were heading in life. She was more concerned about turning them into the strong, independent young women of tomorrow than keeping them the meek, well-behaved little girls of today. And nothing is more central to a young woman's life than settling the question of *master* once and for all.

For my mother, the *master* question was simple. Her heavenly Father, whom she'd walked with and talked with every day from the age of five, was the master of her life. I've never seen anyone express more joy and gratitude for God than my mom. Her love and respect for her Father were infectious. It was hard for anyone to be around her and *not* feel drawn to the Lord of her life. I can't tell you how many teenage girls I've seen come into a saving relationship with Jesus Christ simply because they spent a year getting to know my mother. That's an amazing legacy of faith and one of the things I admire most about her. Everything about her life pointed other people to her master; it was a question she had settled for herself at a young age, and it was the central question she always led other girls to answer for themselves as soon as they could: *Who is going to be the master of your life?*

Second, who will be your mate for life? Mom never failed to remind her girls that we live in a blessed society where women get to choose who they're going to marry. Not every culture is like that. So, since we have the ability to choose, we must do everything we can to make sure we're making the best choice.

As her only daughter, this is something Mom drove into my head all the time. Even back in the 1950s and 1960s, several girls in my mother's Sunday School class either had divorced parents or at least had close family friends or relatives who had been through a painful divorce. And, of course, my mother never forgot the pain and hardship she and her mother went through when her father abandoned them. Sometimes I wondered if her emphasis on choosing a wonderful husband was solely motivated by the emptiness she felt about her own father. Regardless, she wasn't about to let her precious eighth-grade girls walk headlong into a string of bad marriages! She was determined to head off future marriage problems before they ever began by teaching these young ladies how to make the second most important decision of their lives.

She also tried to give the girls a broader perspective on what it means to choose a husband. "It's not *just* about the man himself," she'd say. Several times throughout my teen years, I'd be talking to her about some boy I was dating or interested in, and she'd always ask as many questions about his family as she did about the guy himself. "You're not just marrying a person," she'd say. "You're marrying a *family*, so you want to be sure you know the family really well. You need to feel like that's a family you can be a part of and get along with throughout the years." You better believe her words rang in my ears years later when I started dating John White. I knew he was great, but what about his family? Because of my mother's wise words, I managed to stamp down my infatuation with him long enough to get to know his family a good bit. Once I realized they were as wonderful as he was, I allowed myself to imagine what it would be like to be his wife. Now, after more than forty happy years of marriage, I'm more grateful than ever to my mom for her fierce encouragement in this key area: *Who is going to be your mate for life?*

Third, what will be your mission in life? Mom always tried to get students to look past the present-day dramas of teen life and fix their eyes on where God was leading them. "God has big things in store for you," she'd tell them. "Are you looking for where He's leading?"

Her emphasis on young girls finding God's mission in their lives came back to bite her when her own daughter—*me*—told her I felt called to international missions. At this point, John and

I were married and already had two children at the time. We (and my parents) thought our life mission was settled: John would work with Dad at Chick-fil-A, and I would stay home and raise these wonderful children. God had other plans. And even though this plan wasn't what Mom would have chosen for us, she knew it was up to us to discern our mission. After all, it's what she had taught me and countless other girls for decades: *What will be your mission in life?*

Master, Mate, and Mission. I can't tell you how often these words were thrown around our home. Whenever Mom and Dad had their students over, the conversation always seemed to land on these three key decisions. Whenever Dan, Bubba, and I talked about our future or our desire to make our own decisions, Mom and Dad always brought us back to Master, Mate, and Mission. The concept took on a life of its own around our church, as entire generations were raised knowing The Three Ms.

My friend Julie Cook, who was in Mom's Sunday School class nearly forty years ago, still talks about The Three Ms all the time. She's an accomplished musician, worship leader, and long-time youth choir director, and she tells me that The Three Ms have been part of her ministry since she was thirteen years old. I can't tell you how exciting it is for me to hear that my parents' Sunday School ministry has had such an exponential impact. Julie is only one of who-knows-how-many class alumni that's spread my mother's simple teaching of Master, Mate, and Mission on to entirely new generations of students.

Such a simple teaching, but such a profound message: Who is going to be *master* of your life? Who will be your *mate* for life? What will be your *mission* in life? Mom knew the answers to these three questions will tell you everything you ever need to know about who you are and what kind of life you'll live.

CHAPTER 14

Moving to Tarzan-Land

I had many difficult conversations with my mother over the years, but I don't think any could compare to the news John and I broke to my parents in 1982. We had been in Atlanta with the family for about two years since moving back from Birmingham, Alabama, after graduating college, getting married, and having our first child, Joy. By 1982, we'd had our second child, John IV, and we were settling in for a nice, long life near the family. John was working at Chick-fil-A with Dad by then, and my father was excited about bringing him up in the business alongside my brothers. I was at home with our two small children and all seemed right with the world. After we'd been away for seven years, my mother was happy to have her little girl back home for good. Or so she thought.

During those two years since we'd come back from Birmingham, my husband and I had secretly wrestled with a very unexpected call to full-time Christian service. Specifically, we were struggling with a call to international missions. It's probably more accurate to say that *I* was the one struggling; John knew for sure that's what the Lord was telling us to do. It took me a little longer to come around. However, once we were on the same page and certain this was God's call on our lives, we began the long process of applying to the International Mission Board. For several months, this was our little secret. Neither one of us was ready to break the news to our parents yet—at least until we knew for sure this was going to happen.

Once things started picking up steam, we got more comfortable with the idea of sharing the news. We talked to John's parents first. They lived in Birmingham, so we gave them the news by phone. They weren't surprised at all. In fact, I think the Lord had prepared them for the news. When we told them that we had submitted an application to the International Mission Board, they said they kind of suspected to hear something like that from us someday soon. They'd been to a missionary commissioning service a few weeks prior, and something about that service stuck with them. My father-in-law even commented, "I wouldn't be surprised if we saw John and Trudy do this someday." Little did they know we had already been talking to the mission board at the time. It was a wonderful encouragement to us to hear that they not only accepted and supported the news, but they'd already been expecting it. This experience gave me the boost I needed to finally tell my own parents what was happening.

We decided to share our plans with Mom and Dad soon afterward. I had a hunch that it wouldn't go as smoothly as our talk with John's parents. After all, I'd already been away from home for seven years, and we really seemed to have settled in for the long haul since returning to Atlanta. Chick-fil-A was heading into a decade of explosive growth, and John was right there on the front lines with my father and brothers, seemingly ready to help lead the company into significant years. There's no way Mom and Dad were expecting the news that we were not only planning to leave town but, move to another country. This was going to be a huge curveball for them.

We all sat down one Saturday afternoon around my parents' kitchen table. I can't imagine how many deep, life-changing conversations have taken place around that table. It was the center of so many key decisions in our family, and now it was the place where I had to tell my parents that their little girl was leaving them . . . again. Not only was I leaving, but I was taking my husband—who Dad was excited about raising up in the business—and their two precious grandchildren. And, of course, we thought this would be a lifetime assignment in South America, meaning we'd never live near my parents again. *This is going to be hard*, I thought as we sat down together.

My father's reaction was quick and forceful, as it was with most of his decisions. He said, "Well, Trudy, I'm just going to pray that the Lord closes all these doors." Fair enough. He was certainly entitled to respond and pray however he wanted to. My mother, though, was more thoughtful in her reaction. She honestly didn't say much that day. I could tell she was trying to take it all in before saying anything definitive. She knew her words carried a lot of weight with me, and I think she was trying not to unduly influence what she knew must have been an excruciatingly difficult decision for John and me.

I'm so thankful for that wisdom. The truth is, I'd been putting this conversation off for months for exactly that reason. I needed to be 100 percent sure John and I were doing what was right for our family before I mentioned anything to my mother. If I wasn't certain, I suspected Mom could have talked me out of the decision. I trusted her wisdom and spiritual insight more than anyone else's. I'd spent nearly three decades with her, watching her walk with the Lord and seeing how intimately she knew her heavenly Father. If she had told me missions was a mistake, it could have unraveled all our plans. Thankfully, she had the wisdom to hold her tongue until she'd had time to think, process, and, of course, pray about the news we'd just dropped on them.

I recently uncovered something in my parents' home that makes me wonder if Mom had been quietly preparing for this news for a long time. When I was a young girl, I told my mother that I wanted either to be a missionary or pediatrician when I grew up. Honestly, I only vaguely remember this, and I never once thought about it the entire time leading up to our move to Brazil or during our years spent serving as missionaries. It only recently came to my mind when I found an old notecard among my mother's things. Apparently, she vividly remembered my childhood dreams. After I told her what I wanted to be *someday*, she wrote a few details of our conversation on a notecard and filed it away. I wonder now if she had thought back on that conversation often as I grew up, "pondering it in her heart" (Luke 2:19). Soon after our kitchen conversation, John and I were approved to proceed as career missionaries in Brazil, where John would serve as the treasurer for the largest Southern Baptist mission, working in the local mission office. First, though, we had to go to Fort Worth, Texas, for six months of seminary training before we could take on the assignment. This was a strange time for me and Mom. All the years I was in Birmingham during college and my first few years of marriage, Mom and I talked by phone all the time. She called and visited often, and we hardly felt the three-hour distance between us. That closeness and constant communication continued and even increased after I moved back to Atlanta. However, once I moved to Texas for missions training, our communication just . . . stopped. She never called or wrote. This was 1983, so there was no e-mail, Skype, FaceTime, or text messaging—but the phones worked pretty well! Yet mine never rang, at least not with my mother on the other end. I had no idea what was going on.

Finally, I called and said, "Mom, you never call me anymore! What don't you call? What's wrong?"

She replied, "Well, Trudy, I decided I need to get used to the fact that you're moving to Brazil. And, when you do, I know we won't be able to talk to each other very much. I figured I'd just go ahead and start getting used to that now." It began to dawn on me that Mom was dreaming up quite a strange picture of what my life in Brazil would look like.

Her misinformed ideas came to a head soon afterward when I came home from Fort Worth for a weekend visit. I walked in through the back door into the kitchen and hugged Mom and Dad. We chatted for a few minutes before the stack of books on the kitchen table caught my eye. Usually, Mom's seat at the table was covered with her Bible and Sunday School materials. This day, however, there were books I hadn't seen before. When I stepped over to examine them, I saw that she had checked out several books from the library on Morse code. I also noticed a small Morse code kit, complete with a miniature telegraph box for learning how to tap out messages. I said, "Mom, why on earth are you learning Morse code? Are you planning a new career as a telegraph operator? Are you on your way to prison and need to learn how to tap out secret messages? What's going on?"

Slightly annoyed at my ribbing, she said, "No, Trudy. I got these books so I could learn how to talk to you while you're in Brazil." I was stunned.

"What do you mean?" I asked. "How are we going to talk by Morse code?"

She replied, "I don't know! I'm just trying to get ready for when you move away from telephones and civilization!"

Clearly, Mom and I needed to have a talk about what modern life was like in Brazil. I came to realize she had this terrifying picture of me, John, and our two children living in a dirt hut in the middle of a jungle, unable to talk by phone and getting around town only by swinging from vines like Tarzan. I suppose, somewhere in her mental picture of the dangerous, uncivilized, and untamed wilderness of Brazil, she imagined telegram wires running from hut to hut for tapping out messages in Morse code.

"Mom! For heaven sakes!" I laughed. "We aren't moving into a treehouse like Swiss Family Robinson! We're moving to *Rio de Janeiro*. It's a modern city and has pretty much anything you'd find in most American cities. There are roads, cars, office buildings, postal service, television, and—*yes*—even telephones! We can talk whenever we want to!" Fortunately, that put her mind at ease and things got a little easier for us both. I love that she started learning Morse code for me, though. It's the perfect picture of my mother as the consummate problem-solver. She didn't ask anyone for help; she just identified what she thought would be a problem and started thinking of ways to solve it.

A few months later, John and I were in the final stages of our preparation and the mission agency, based in Richmond, Virginia, set a date for our commissioning service. Both our families flew up to celebrate with us in Richmond. John's parents, Mom, Dad, my brothers, and my sisters-in-law all met us there and we had a wonderful time of dedication. It meant the world to me to have my parents there, even though I knew they were hurting a little more every day leading up to our departure. Dad was mostly quiet;

I could tell he was struggling with our move. Mom, however, was a rock of support. She'd often wondered aloud about which of her grandchildren would be called into the pastorate or some other form of full-time ministry service. Little did she know it would be her own daughter.

Her support carried me all the way to the airport the day we were set to fly off for what we expected to be a lifetime of service in Brazil. Seeing my husband and children sitting with all our bags packed at the airport was even hard for me. As far as I knew, I was going to spend the rest of my life in another country, far away from the family who had meant so much to me for so long. It was an emotional day for all of us. Gratefully, this was back in the time before airport security was as strict as it is today. Friends and family members were allowed to walk travelers all the way up to the gate, sending them off with hugs and kisses immediately before they boarded the plane. I'm so glad that was the case, because I needed my mother that day. I needed her sweet smile, words of encouragement, and faith that everything was going to be okay. And she was there to deliver all of it.

When it was time to board the plane for Brazil, Mom was right by my side. Dad, however, was nowhere to be found. He'd wandered off to a different part of the airport terminal to grieve our leaving. "It's all just a bit hard for him," Mom said. "You know he loves you and will support you every step of the way. He just couldn't say goodbye." With tears streaming down both our faces, Mom and I squeezed each other as tightly as we could, said goodbye, and finally let each other go. I walked through the doors of the gate and down the boarding bridge to the plane. Even though I couldn't see her through the window of the plane, I know she was standing there, wiping away tears and waving as our plane took off for what she had imaged to be Tarzan-land.

CHAPTER 15

Grandbabies in Brazil

aving goodbye to her daughter, son-in-law, and two grand-children was hard for my mother. She put up a brave face and never once mentioned how difficult it was for her, but I knew she was having a really hard time with our leaving. Fortunately, we weren't dependent on Morse code communication as she originally feared. We spoke often by phone, and we discovered a new love for letter-writing. Mom wrote us all the time, crafting sweet letters of prayer and encouragement and keeping us informed on everything that was happening back home. I could just picture her sitting at her little kitchen table with her Bible and Sunday School lesson pushed to the side, crafting each letter with love and care.

Our mail was delivered to John at the mission office, and I was thrilled whenever he brought home a new letter from my parents. Things really picked up, though, when we each got a fax machine.

Remember, this was a time before email. Back then, writing a letter meant writing an *actual* letter, folding it up, sticking it in an envelope, slapping a stamp on the outside, and dropping it in the mail. It could take a week or two for a letter to make the journey from Atlanta to Campinas, São Paulo, where we were studying our first year for language school. The fax machine—cutting-edge technology in the 1980s—gave us instant communication for the first time. It was a miracle! We got Mom a fax machine for home and we had one in the mission office. That meant, for the first time, she could write a note to me, John, or the children and instantly deliver it to us thousands of miles away. Oh, the wonders of technology!

As much as we enjoyed the letters, we all got much more excited about Mom and Dad's annual trips to Brazil. No matter how busy Dad was, he carved out two weeks almost every year around New Years to make the overnight flight to our little home in Campinas or Rio. I can't describe how excited the children got about these visits. My son John, who was only two when we first moved there, still remembers the sheer excitement he felt as Grandmother and Granddad's visit neared. I remember it too. I loved the work we were doing in Brazil, but I missed my parents desperately. I'd lived apart from them for many years when I lived in Birmingham, but this was different. It was as if Mom and I could *feel* every one of the 4,500 miles that separated us during those years. I felt my whole spirit perk up when I knew she was coming to see me.

Because of the travel and luggage issues, Mom had to get creative about the gifts she brought the children. She never wanted to come without special treasures, but her gifts required a whole new dimension of thought and preparation. One year, she found a set of cardboard blocks that came flat and had to be folded up into red boxes or "bricks." She thought that gift was a gold mine She filled an entire suitcase with these flat sheets of cardboard that she could magically transform into a large set of blocks for the children when they arrived at our home. The set looked massive when fully assembled, but she made it fit into the bags she already had. She was a master at finding creative solutions to intimidating problems. I'm so grateful she used that problem-solving artistry to make my children feel so loved. They never forgot that special Christmas gift.

Of course, she did have a to get used to a few other things about our life in Brazil. The first time they came to visit, for example, John and I were still in language school in Campinas. That area was less developed and a little rougher than where we'd eventually end up, but it's where we needed to be to learn the language. We were intensely focused on learning Portuguese that year; after all, our entire ministry career depended on us being able to speak the language!

We arrived there in April 1984, and Mom and Dad came for their first two-week visit that December. John and I had spent those eight months getting comfortable in our new environment, making new friends, learning the culture, and generally making ourselves at home there. Dropping my mother and father into that environment, though, was a bit of a culture shock for them. Seeing the poor living conditions in some areas worried them, but they managed to keep level heads and never said anything to question where we were or what we were doing. Well . . . *almost* never.

When they arrived in town for their first visit, John and I wanted to take them out to dinner to catch up. At that time, we had a wonderful local woman helping us in our home and with the children every day while John and I were in school. Cleuza was a fine Christian lady, and we had grown to love her and her family dearly. She was raising five children of her own, and they were the perfect playmates for Joy and young John. Of course, neither she nor her children spoke any English and our communication was sometimes a challenge, but we trusted her completely with our son and daughter.

Cleuza and her family lived in a different part of town from where we were. John and I lived in a small, humble house that year, but it looked like a castle compared to Cleuza's home. Her house was small and cramped with seven people, and it had dirt floors and—believe it or not—no interior walls. They separated their living room from their sleeping areas with simple sheets, something most American families couldn't imagine. John and I couldn't help them much financially, but we were happy to pay her for her work and enjoy the time we spent with them. By the time my parents came to visit, we thought nothing about dropping our children off in front of Cleuza's home to play. It felt no different than dropping them off at a friend's house in suburban Atlanta.

My parents, however, were not prepared for this. The night we took them out to dinner, John and I had arranged for Cleuza to keep our children in her home for the night. We piled Mom and Dad in the car with us and made the journey to the other part of town. As we chatted in the car, I could tell Mom and Dad were keeping mental tabs on the surrounding area we were driving through. The longer we talked, the poorer and more desolate the neighborhoods out the windows became. When we finally stopped in front of Cleuza's house, John and I didn't even get out of the car. We simply opened the doors and told Joy and John to have a good time. They joyfully ran off toward Cleuza's excited children as Mom and Dad's jaws dropped. I'm sure they were thinking, *You can't be serious! You're going to leave my grandchildren here?*

To their credit, Mom and Dad never questioned our parenting decisions and seemed to trust that we knew what we were doing. I knew that moment was a huge culture shock for them, though. I think it told them everything they needed to know about the kind of life John and I were going to give their grandchildren in Brazil. And, throughout that first visit, my parents got to know Cleuza and her children a bit. Her little ones grew to love Mom and Dad and seemed nearly as excited about seeing them as my own children. Apparently, Brazilian children were just as drawn to my parents as the boys and girls in their little Georgia church!

A year later, after we had moved to Rio de Janeiro, I became pregnant with our third child. Mom and I kept in touch throughout the pregnancy and, as the delivery date approached, I asked my mother if she could come spend a few weeks with me in Brazil for the birth. It dawned on me early in the pregnancy that I'd never been through this without my mother. Our first child, Joy, was born when we lived in Birmingham and Mom drove over and spent two or three weeks with us to help with whatever we needed. Then, by the time John was born, we had moved back to Atlanta and Mom was there with us every day to help with the baby and spend time with little Joy. Now, I was facing my third delivery and I desperately wanted my mother to be there just as she had been before. Even though Mom had never made the trip from the states alone, she didn't hesitate. "Of course, I'll come!" she said. "I wouldn't miss it!"

Mom arrived that September just prior to my due date. We lived in an apartment in a Rio high-rise building then, and Mom made herself right at home. In fact, she even started to get to know our neighbors during that visit and ultimately became life-long friends with the missionary couple who lived a floor above us. That was my mother—building deep, meaningful, long-term relationships wherever she went. I've honestly never seen anything like it.

Mom kept herself busy in those days before the baby arrived. Our apartment was tiny, and we hadn't quite figured out where to put a new baby. So, Mom helped me clear out the apartment's small storage area and turn it into a makeshift nursery. In typical Jeannette Cathy fashion, however, she wasn't satisfied with the idea of sticking her grandbaby in a closet. Dreaming of how to make it a special space for a child, Mom did what came naturally: she started painting. She'd recently discovered a love for painting landscapes and had a particular knack for capturing the beauty and majesty of the sky and clouds. By the time the baby arrived, Mom had painted an amazing mural on the little nursery wall, giving our new little girl a beautiful sky to look at as she laid in her crib. One of my favorite photographs of Mom shows her standing on a ladder in our apartment, sweating from Rio's September heat and smiling as she painted a masterpiece for her granddaughter. That picture says so much about who she was and how much she loved her family.

Soon after the mural was complete, I went into labor and was blessed to have Mom stay with my other two children as we welcomed our second daughter into the world. We hadn't told Mom yet, but John and I had already decided that we wanted to honor my mother by naming this child after her. Imagine her joy as we introduced her to Angela Jeannette White. It was a perfect moment for our family. Yes, we were thousands of miles from the rest of the family, but Mom made us feel right next door. Her love had a way of closing any gap.

This whole scene was repeated a few years later when our fourth child, David, was born. Once again, Mom packed up and moved down to Brazil for several weeks to be with me and help us get ready for the new arrival. I've had four children in all—one born in Alabama, one born in Georgia, and two born in Rio de Janeiro—and I've been so incredibly blessed to have my mother there with me for each one. No matter where I was on planet Earth, my mother made me and my children a priority. That created an unbreakable bond between her and my four children that bridged any distance during my family's twenty-two-year missionary service. My sons and daughters knew from birth that anywhere my mother was felt like *home*.

CHAPTER 16

Joy's Polka-Dotted Birthday Party

*J*ohn and I were back home with our children on a missionary furlough the month our daughter Joy turned twelve. The family was so excited! We'd been in Brazil for eight years or so at that point, so we all treasured the moments we were able to spend on my parents' farm. Mom was especially thrilled. She loved spending quality time with each of her twelve grandchildren, and it had been difficult for her to have four of the twelve so far away. Despite the lengths she went in order to make my children feel loved, known, and included in the family during her two-week-long New Years trips to Brazil, the nearly five-thousand-mile distance weighed heavily on her at times. She hated any sense of separation within the family, so she went out of her way to create special memories when we were all together. Joy's twelfth birthday was going to be one of those times.

Mom had been planning it for a while. She made sure Dan and Bubba's families would be there, ensuring the three Cathy children, their spouses, and the dozen cousins would all be under the same roof for a day of fun. We'd taken those times for granted before our move to Brazil, but now we knew how valuable it was to be together as one big family. Mom had also cleaned and decorated the house, planned the meal, and made sure she had Joy's favorite cake ready to go. Every time I saw or talked to Mom for the week or two leading up to the party, she told me what she was planning and asked me if I thought Joy would like it. Even though Mom's total focus was on giving Joy and the family a wonderful experience, I could tell it meant the world to her having her entire family—three generations—all together for the first time in a while. A couple of days before the party, Mom was ready to burst! As far as she was concerned, *nothing* was going to interfere with this party. It was a train racing down the tracks, and it could not be stopped.

But (you *had* to see the *but* coming) there was a problem—and that problem was written all over Joy's face. The afternoon before her birthday extravaganza, Joy started feeling bad. She didn't have much of an appetite and felt a little feverish. That night, her skin started itching terribly. We sent her to bed with some Tylenol and Benadryl and hoped for the best, praying it was just her allergies overreacting to Atlanta's spring weather and infamous pollen. It wasn't. The next morning—the day of the party—Joy woke up with little red dots all over her face and body. Chicken pox had exploded all over her like a fireworks spectacular in celebration of her birthday. She was itchy and miserable. More than that, though, she was bitterly disappointed. "I guess you better call Grandmother and tell her I can't come," she said as she wiped away a tear. "I look terrible."

My heart broke for both Joy and my mother. I couldn't bear the thought of Joy having to stay home with either me or John while the rest of the family got together for a rare all-family event. I also couldn't bear the thought of telling Mom the birthday girl couldn't come to her own party. What terrible timing!

I called Mom and let her know what was going on. She felt horrible about Joy's discomfort, but she immediately went into the typical Jeannette Cathy problem-solving mode. While the rest of us were bemoaning the fact that Joy would have to stay home, that thought never even occurred to my mother. Ninety-nine percent of the population (including me at the time) would think, *Can we still have the party?* but my mother's immediate reaction was, *How can we still have the party?* Quitting wasn't an option for my mother, especially not when a precious grandchild's tender heart was on the line.

Mom said, "Trudy, if Joy feels like coming, she is always welcome in my home, chicken pox or not. This is *her* party. Plan on bringing her over, and I'll figure out the rest." I said okay, and Mom went to work. She called my sisters-in-law to let them know what was going on and to warn anyone who *hadn't* already had the chicken pox. We obviously didn't want to cause a family-wide chicken pox outbreak, but Mom refused to rob Joy of her birthday party. Even if it would just be Mom and Joy, that party was *going* to happen as far as my mother was concerned.

Fortunately for us, most of the family had either had the chicken pox already or were willing to risk being in the same house with Joy's itchy welts. Joy was still feeling a little insecure about her appearance, though. She *was* a twelve-year-old girl, after all. She hadn't seen the whole family in months, and now she was going to walk in covered head to toe in little red polka dots? "This is so embarrassing," she said as John and I piled our children in the car. "Everybody's going to stare at me the whole time!"

When we got to the farmhouse, we pulled up to the carport in the back of the house at the kitchen door. Mom saw us out the kitchen window and ran out to greet us with the biggest smile on her face. She yelled, "Happy birthday!" and held her arms open wide to welcome Joy. Immediately, Joy broke out in the happiest, biggest laugh we'd heard from her in a while. When I looked up at my mother in the doorway, I could see why. Mom's face and arms were completely covered . . . in little red dots. She'd taken a tube of bright red lipstick and marked up her face and arms in fake chicken pox to make Joy feel better. It was one of the sweetest things I've ever seen.

As we walked into the kitchen, we were greeted with an entire family of Cathy children and grandchildren covered in little red dots. Mom had gone through the whole family, marking each one with their own set of bright, smeary, ruby red chicken pox. "You'll have to excuse us, Joy, but we've all got the chicken pox today," she said. "But we've decided to have your party anyway."

Mom did so many things over the years to make my children feel special, from the sentimental to the downright silly. This one, though, is extra special. It was like a magic trick, watching my mother transform an awkward twelve-year-old girl's discomfort and embarrassment into one of our family's favorite memories. None of us will ever forget Joy's polka-dotted, chicken-pox birthday party—or how special Mom made her feel on what could have been the worst day of her life.

CHAPTER 17

The Queen of Reduce, Reuse, Recycle

*I*n 1985, my parents took their love of children to the next level by launching WinShape Camps, a faith-based, overnight summer camp experience for boys and girls on the campus of Berry College in Mt. Berry, Georgia. The summers I spent at camp as a young girl changed the whole course of my life, and I always came home telling my parents all about the exciting moments I shared with friends and heartfelt conversations I had with my counselors. I was overjoyed when they took the bold step of launching a brand-new camp to serve a new generation of children!

Mom and Dad were far more than the camp's distant, mysterious benefactors. They absolutely loved dropping by the camp and spending time with the boys and girls who showed up every session. These were children from every walk of life. Some came from well-off homes, while others came from families who struggled financially. Money was never an object for WinShape campers, though. If a child wanted to come and needed help, WinShape Camps was there to help them. That meant some of the boys and girls who showed up came without a change of clothes or what most of us would call the basic necessities. Whenever Mom found a few of these girls, she'd pile them all in the car and take them on a shopping trip.

Now, I want you to picture this through the eyes of a twelve-year-old girl. When they heard they were going on a shopping trip with Jeannette Cathy, the wife Chick-fil-A's founder, they got excited. I mean, they were *pumped*. These young girls rarely got to go to a mall, and most of them spent their days dressed head to toe in either hand-me-downs or discount-store clothes. The thought of a shopping trip with a well-to-do woman always fired them up!

You can imagine their surprise, then, when their magical, exciting car ride with my mother led them not to the mall or a department store . . . but to the front door of Walmart. "Uh, Mrs. Cathy," they'd sometimes eke out, "I thought we were going to the mall. What are we doing here?"

Mom would laugh and say, "The mall? Why on earth would we go to the mall? We can find everything we need right here. This is where Truett and I do most of our shopping!"

She wasn't kidding. My parents were not what you'd imagine when you picture the founders of one of America's most successful companies. I wouldn't call them *cheap*, but . . . well, let's just call them *frugal*. Remember, my parents were born in the early 1920s, and they both struggled with their families through the Great Depression. If your parents or grandparents lived through those difficult times, you might have noticed a certain thriftiness in them too. Living through an economic collapse at that level leaves a scar that never fully heals, no matter how much time passes or how much success you achieve later in life. For my parents, who both grew up with next to nothing, Walmart jeans were the height of luxury!

I've mentioned how my parents were always content to live in their little farmhouse, no matter how well off they became. I've also mentioned how my mother always tried to fix broken vacuums and kitchen appliances. That wasn't *just* because she couldn't get much help out on the farm or because she enjoyed fiddling with things; it was because she didn't want to buy a replacement! If she could save $20 by fixing a ten-year-old toaster instead of buying a new one, she would. I don't mean she only did this when they were younger and the business was new; this was when she was ninety years old and could have purchased anything she ever wanted. Chick-fil-A was a booming national brand at this point, but she was still trying to fix a broken heating coil in a toaster oven!

As Mom got older, she slowed down and finally started to let the guys on the farm help her take care of little things around the house. Chris Phillips, the farmhand I mentioned earlier who stumbled upon the charred remains of Dad's centerpiece inferno, found himself faced with a few flat-out ridiculous repair requests. When something would break, Mom would often leave it on her kitchen counter with a note, asking Chris or one of the other guys to fix it. One morning, Chris came in to find a coffee mug on the counter. This was not a special mug. It wasn't ornate or expensive, and it held no sentimental meaning to my parents. It was, in every respect, an average, basic, dime-a-dozen coffee mug she had probably bought twenty years earlier at Walmart. Anyway, the handle had broken off—either from a fall or, more likely, it had simply given up after nine million cups of coffee spanning two decades. Rather than tossing the broken mug in the trash and using one of the other dozen mugs in the cabinet, Mom set the mug on the counter with the handle and two tubes of epoxy sticking out of it. Right in front was a note that simply said, "Fix this cup." It still had a lot of life left in it as far as she was concerned. "Why replace what can still be fixed?" she'd say. Chris sadly didn't have a chance to reattach the broken handle to the mug before Mom died. So, in honor of her, we left the broken mug, handle, glue, and note sitting on the kitchen counter right where she left it. She's been gone several years now, but I just saw that broken mug this morning. It still makes me smile.

At least one time, Chris had to push back on Mom's repair requests. She'd bought a plastic watering can for her indoor flowers a couple of years earlier, and it sprang a leak. She brought it to him and said, "Chris, this is leaking somewhere. Can you figure out what's wrong and fix it?"

He smiled and said, "Mrs. Jeannette, I think this one is a goner. I saw these at Walmart for two bucks the other day. Let's just get you a new one this time, okay?"

Repairing what was broken wasn't the only way Mom tried to save a dollar here and there. She also repurposed what most of us would consider to be trash. My son John remembers a time when he was a boy and we were home from Brazil on furlough. He noticed a few large, disposable foil pans sitting on the counter and asked her about them. She said, "Oh, John, just look at these pans! Aren't they great? A friend brought some food over the other day and delivered it in these foil pans. I just couldn't throw them out. I mean, who would bring food over and leave these pans behind like they were nothing? I can get a lot of use out of them!"

That's right: my mother couldn't stop raving about a set of cheap, disposable, aluminum foil pans. That was probably thirty years ago. I figure there's a decent chance those pans are still in that kitchen somewhere.

One of the funniest acts of repurposing had to be her make-shift notepaper. I was cleaning out part of my parents' house recently and came across a set of notes Mom had made during her personal Bible study. Only her notes weren't on loose-leaf paper. And they weren't in a notebook, on index cards, or on a legal pad. No, this particular stack of notes was made up of strange sheets of white cardboard just a little smaller than a sheet of regular paper. I couldn't for the life of me figure out what it was. Blank white cereal box? No, it was too thick for that. Old Chick-fil-A shipping boxes? No, it was too thin. *What is this?* I wondered for the longest time. A while later, I was unpacking a new pair of pantyhose I'd recently purchased. The hose were packaged and wrapped around a thin, blank, white piece of cardboard a little smaller than a sheet of paper. *Good gracious*, I realized. *Mom saved the backing from her pantyhose packages and turned it into notepaper!* Who else but my mother would make insightful, prayer-filled, deeply spiritual Bible study notes on the packaging from her underwear? No one.

My mother was the most generous, caring woman I've ever met. She'd do anything for anyone, and she always gave more to others than she ever got for herself. But, my goodness, I've never seen anyone stretch a dime as far as she could. It could have been irritating at times . . . if it wasn't just so funny to watch.

CHAPTER 18

The Chicken Pin

One Christmas morning in the 1970s, Mom opened a small, simply wrapped gift that has since become a treasured family heirloom. It was early in the growth of Chick-fil-A as a business, and at this point Dad had already opened seventeen mall locations across the country. It had been a hard-fought battle to get the business off the ground, growing far beyond the simple Dwarf House that had been part of their lives for nearly thirty years. Mom and Dad had both made a lot of sacrifices to build something they believed in. The hardest sacrifice either of them made, though, was time with each other. Even after decades of marriage, they still loved spending time together, and we could all tell how much Mom missed him when he wasn't home.

That Christmas, Dad wanted to do something to honor all the sacrifices Mom had made for Chick-fil-A. He visited a jeweler with a simple sketch and an idea for a special gift. He wanted to create a unique diamond pin in the shape of the C from the Chick-fil-A logo. The body of the letter would be filled with diamonds—one for every Chick-fil-A location (seventeen at that point). The four red chicken combs on top of the C would be rubies, giving the whole thing a classy yet distinctive look. Anyone who saw it could tell it was the Chick-fil-A logo, but you could also tell it was especially meaningful. It was a true, one-of-a-kind creation, and Dad was so excited to present it to Mom.

When she opened it that Christmas morning, her eyes sparkled brighter than the diamonds on the pendant. She knew it was more than a trinket or last-minute gift idea. She could immediately see how much the pin meant to my father, and she instinctively knew what the gift represented. Together, they were building a business that would, in many ways, change the food industry and certainly our family forever. All the hard work, late nights, early mornings, and missed dinners were represented by the curve of diamonds twinkling in the little jewelry box. This wasn't an "I'm sorry" gift from an absent husband to a frustrated wife; no, this was something much more significant. This was a thank-you from one business partner to another, in recognition of the fact that Chick-fil-A would not have been what it was at the time—or become what it is today—without the grace, kindness, patience, and contribution of Jeannette Cathy. With that pin, he was officially crowning her the First Lady of Chick-fil-A.

Mother was a simple woman and wore very little jewelry. Rather than a stuffed jewelry box filled to the brim with bracelets, bangles, and broaches, she had only a handful of pieces, and each one meant something significant to her. Except for her wedding set, I don't think any of those pieces meant as much to her as that little Chick-fil-A pin. Somehow, Dad managed to pack thirty years of meaning into one diamond-studded C. It was her badge of honor, her medal of valor for a life of service to others and a life of commitment to her husband. It is impossible to describe how much that pin meant to her. For the next twenty years, she was often seen at business events and store openings with that sparkling Chick-fil-A logo pinned to her dress.

Fast forward to a new Chick-fil-A restaurant's grand opening in the late 1990s. I had been asked to speak at its dedication dinner, and I was feeling anxious about it. Ever since Dad opened his first mall location in Atlanta, the company had used these dedication dinners to commemorate the owner-operator's achievement and to set the right expectations for his or her team members. Originally, Dad personally attended each store dedication and gave a little speech. He used the opportunity to dedicate the location to the Lord and to make sure the operator and team members knew that it was the Lord—not Truett Cathy or even the customers—that they were really serving. His goal from the start was for each Chick-fil-A location to become a powerful, positive influence in its community, so he always stressed in these dedication speeches how important it was to serve the Lord and serve our customers with the highest level of excellence. Of course, he also stressed how fun it was to work at Chick-fil-A and encouraged the owner-operator and the new team to find ways to make the restaurant a fun place to be for both employees and guests. Every dedication dinner means the world to the teams involved; these are nights the operators never forget, and Dad was always there to give them the motivational speech of their lives.

Over the years, as Dad got older and as my brothers grew into their leadership roles within the company, Dan and Bubba started attending these dedication dinners and giving the speech on behalf of Chick-fil-A and the Cathy family. John and I had been away in Brazil during that transition, so I hadn't personally delivered a dedication speech. Once we moved back to the states and settled in Richmond, Virginia, I had the opportunity to get a little more involved with the business here and there. One specific way was for me to rotate the dedication dinner responsibilities alongside Dan and Bubba. It was a way to share the load, which was increasingly important during that season of the company's growth. It seemed like we opened a new store every week back then! I was happy to get more involved and to help my brothers, so I jumped at the chance.

My first dedication dinner speech was for a longtime friend and mentor, Wayne Farr. Wayne is the Operator who had trained me more than twenty years earlier when I was preparing to open my own Chick-fil-A restaurant. He was now opening his fifth location, and we thought this would be a great way for me to start doing dedication speeches. I planned what I wanted to say and checked with Dan and Bubba to see what they said in their talks to make sure we were all on the same page and giving a consistent message to the different store Operators I was fully prepared, excited, and ready for business—until I found out my parents were going to be there.

When I got word a few days before the event that my parents would be among the attendees, my confidence and excitement turned to fear and anxiety. There I was, a grown forty-something-year-old woman, mother of four, former Chick-fil-A Operator, and successful career missionary, but I was scared to give a ten-minute talk in front of my own father. How ridiculous! The fear grew worse leading up to the dinner. When I arrived and saw my parents, I felt my heart sink to my stomach, bringing with it a fresh crop of butterflies to contend with. I had no idea why I was so nervous, but, for some reason, doing *that* talk in front of my father was the most intimidating thing in the world to me. *He's the master! He's the founder of Chick-fil-A!* I thought. *Why would these people want to hear from me when Truett Cathy himself is sitting right there in the crowd?*

I excused myself to the restroom to compose myself. My mother could sense that something was wrong and followed me back there. When she walked in, I was standing at the sink trying to pull myself together. I just looked at her and said, "Mom, do you think Dad should do this talk? I mean, he's already here. It seems weird to have *me* do this instead of *him*. I'm sure everyone would rather hear from him, anyway." It's funny how, even in my mid-forties, I found myself running back to my mother for her wisdom and advice. I'm so glad I did on that particular night.

She looked me straight in the eyes and said, "Trudy, you can do this. You're going to be great, and your father is going to be so proud of you!" And then she did something I never expected. Without a second thought, she took the diamond Chick-fil-A pin off her lapel. The pin that she'd worn for two decades. The pin that represented the love, care, and sacrifice she and my father had shared for fifty years at that point. The pin that celebrated her as the First Lady of Chick-fil-A. "Here," she continued. "You put this on, and you go out there and speak with the confidence of the Lord. He is with you, Trudy. And so am I."

I don't know if I have ever loved my mother more than I did at that moment. She communicated so much in that one loving gesture. It wasn't merely a pep talk for a single speaking engagement; I could feel her encouraging me as I tentatively stepped my toes back into the waters of the family business. It was as though she was saying, "Trudy, I know you're worried that you've been away a long time. I know you're still trying to find your place in all this now that you're back. You'll figure it out. Your brothers have their roles, and you have yours. We *all* have our parts to play, and every one of us is important. Never forget who you are—or *whose* you are."

Needless to say, I came out of that bathroom a much different person than I was when I went into it. When it was time to give the dedication speech, I did what my mother told me to do: I spoke in the confidence of the Lord. That was such a powerful night for me in so many ways. Sure, I got to do something meaningful for my longtime friend and mentor, Wayne. But, more than that, I had a perfect moment in time with my mother. In the most unexpected time and place—a *bathroom*, no less—Mom lifted me up when I needed her most. And in giving me her pin (which she told me to keep from then on), I could feel her passing the torch to me just as Dad had passed it to my brothers. It was a significant moment for my family, and it was a night I'll never forget.

The "passing of the pin" took on an even deeper meaning for me a just few years ago. It was 2015, and my son-in-law Brent was celebrating the grand opening of his first restaurant, Chick-fil-A Greystone in Birmingham. Brent and my daughter Angela were thrilled to stake their claim in the business; they are one of the many third-generation family members stepping into key roles throughout the company. Dad had passed away before Brent's restaurant opened, which left a dark cloud over the dedication ceremony. However, Mom was still excited to make the trip to Birmingham to celebrate Angela and Brent and to lend her support to their new business.

I was honored to speak at Angela and Brent's dedication dinner, but I did this one a little differently than I ever had. For the first time, I brought my mother up front with me. Together, we told the crowd about the pin and what all it represented for our family. Then, we asked Angela to join us. Tears started rolling down her face when she realized what was about to happen. With her little, shaking hands, Mom reached up and took the pin off of me and, with a few words of love and encouragement to her granddaughter, she proudly pinned it to Angela's lapel—something Mom and I planned on doing all along. Everyone erupted in applause as three generations of Cathy ladies held each other crying, passing a priceless family heirloom down to the next generation.

Mom always viewed that pin first and foremost through the eyes of a wife. To her, it was a gift from her husband and held special meaning because of the love and commitment it represented. That little chicken pin means something else to the rest of us, though. When we see it, we don't see a husband, father, or founder of Chick-fil-A. Instead, we see *her*. We see her endless patience. We see her grace under fire. We see her kindness, generosity, faith, longsuffering, encouragement, and support. Above all, we see her limitless love for her family and her unwavering conviction that we can overcome any obstacle and achieve any victory "in the confidence of the Lord." That pin is no longer a husband's thank-you for a few years of sacrifice; it's a monument to an entire life of service. And it's one that our family will wear proudly for generations to come.

CHAPTER 19

Painting Her Heart Out

By the time Mom turned sixty-five, she really needed a new hobby. My brothers and I had been gone for a while, and Dad was still spending every day at work. The farm felt awfully big and lonely for her during the day. After a lifetime celebrating the arts through music and dancing, I suppose it's only natural that her latest area of interest was an as-yet unexplored artistic endeavor: oil painting.

In typical Jeannette Cathy fashion, she decided to teach herself how to paint. Sure, it might have been easier to take lessons, but my mother always felt oddly confident about her ability to teach herself new things. What's even more surprising is that she was almost always right. She had taught herself many new tricks and trades over the years from gardening to appliance repair. And let's not forget that she could pick up just about any instrument and figure out the basics in no time at all. How much harder could painting be?

Apparently, not much harder at all. Mom immediately took to the craft. She started by driving herself to the local arts and crafts store for supplies, picking up some canvases, oils, brushes, and one or two art books for reference. She spent a little time studying different techniques, but mainly, she just dove in head first and started painting. Her early works are incredible; you'd never know they were the works of a first-year artist who'd never painted a day in her life. She started with nature scenes, painting the beauty of God's creation the way she'd always pictured it in her mind.

My sister-in-law Cindy recently told me, "I distinctly remember her painting a sky with clouds. I thought, *That's not what clouds and the sky look like. They don't look that dramatic. Why did she paint the sky such a deep blue?* After that, I started noticing the reality of the sky—and she was right. She painted the clouds exactly as they appeared; I had just never paid attention to them before. Through her paintings, she made me really notice the beauty of the sky. She saw more than I did, and she painted it perfectly."

As stunning as her nature scenes were, she really surprised us when she started painting people. Somehow, she was able to instinctively capture every curve, line, and wrinkle of the human face in her art. She mixed her oils into perfect skin tones and shadows, and she managed to inject genuine emotion into the eyes of her subjects. There are three paintings in particular that surprised even her. She hung them in her living room, where they're still on display today. She called these three *her ladies* because they each feature a close-up view of an older woman. One shows a woman in partial profile looking over a balcony at the busy world below. Her far-off stare is captivating; you can't help but wonder what she's thinking about. The wrinkles, sagging skin, and neatly combed white hair show that she's had a rich lifetime of experience, and her sweet, tight-lipped smile denotes a peace about what she's overcome and what still lies ahead. In a way, I think Mom was painting her own future with each brushstroke.

Her other two *ladies* are even more remarkable. One is of an older woman in tattered clothes. Her coat sleeve is fraying at the edges and the scarf around her head is clearly old and wellworn. What stands out to everyone, though, is her beautiful smile. Mom loved to point it out to others. She'd say of this *lady*, "No, she didn't have much. Even her clothes are old and worn. But look at her beautiful smile! Whatever hardship she's been through couldn't rob her of her smile!" It was as though my mother was describing a photograph of an old friend.

Mom's third *lady* is what gets most people's attention. It shows a tight closeup of an older woman's face surrounded completely in black, the way a photographer might use a black backdrop to bring total focus and attention to his subject's face. At first glance, most people think this painting actually *is* a photograph. The shading, use of light and shadow, blend of skin tones, and perfectly placed hand on the old woman's chin is striking. Her lips are slightly parted by a knowing grin, giving the impression that she's just figured out a secret about you (but has decided to keep it to herself). And then there are her eyes. Those eyes! It's the first thing you notice when you walk into the room. You immediately feel her presence and her sparkling, penetrating stare. It's amazing, nearly every visitor has commented on how she seems to follow you across the room with those eyes. This one truly was Mom's masterpiece.

From age sixty-five to around eighty, Mom spent most of her free time in the little art studio she made out of my childhood bedroom. She painted nature scenes, flowers, people, family, friends, swans, and anything else that sparked her imagination. Many of these paintings still hang in the old farmhouse today. A precious few were given as gifts to the special people in her life. Julie Cook, one of Mom's Sunday School girls whom I mentioned earlier, told me about a special present Mom made for her mother. Julie's mom was the organist at the church where we were members. The church was celebrating her twenty-five years of devoted service, and Mom wanted to add something to the celebration. So, she created a wonderful painting of Julie's mother sitting at her organ giving her gifts to the Lord. Julie says that her mother can't think of mine without remembering that precious gift.

"I've already told my mother that I want that painting one day," Julie said. "I want it because *Mrs. Cathy* painted it. How sweet is it to have my beloved Sunday School teacher paint a picture of my mother at the organ bench? That will always be an incredible way for me to remember them *both*."

My mother didn't only give her art away, she also used it as an opportunity to spend special time with some of her grandchildren. For example, when my son John was in fourth grade, we came back from Brazil for a few weeks on furlough and stayed in a small guest house on the farm. John had an art project due for school at that time, and he was excited by his grandmother's offer to help.

"I ran over there every day to work on my painting," he recalls. "I wanted to paint a Lamborghini, but I didn't know how. So, Grandmother taught me how to set up my canvas, make a light sketch in pencil first, and mix the oils. She taught me about perspective and how to mix light and dark colors to show depth. We spent several whole days together in her little studio room, and by the time we went back to Brazil, I had a white Lamborghini she and I were both proud of!" I loved watching John run over to spend that time with Mom every day. It was the perfect opportunity for them to share a special moment they'd both remember forever. In fact, I still have that white Lamborghini painting, and Mom and John were right. It's perfect.

My niece Rachel, Bubba and Cindy's daughter, had a similar week with my mother years later as a young adult. Rachel had spent years living away from home in China and then in California. By this time, she was in her mid-twenties and working for Chick-fil-A on the West Coast. Mom knew Rachel had a deep appreciation for art, so she gave Rachel her very first sketch book. It was a precious, meaningful gift to Rachel—mainly because Mom had taken such an interest in what she was doing. Even though she had twelve grandchildren and was starting to get a full crop of great-grandchildren, Mom *always* strove to stay current on what each child and grandchild was up to. When she saw Rachel developing a love for art, Mom knew that would be a way to deepen their connection.

Rachel loved the gift *and* the heart behind it. She took her sketchbook back home to California and immediately started filling it up with drawings. She sketched fruit, tables, nature scenes, and anything else that caught her eye. When she created something she was especially proud of, she'd mail it back to her grandmother in Georgia so the two could discuss it and so Mom could see how Rachel's artwork was progressing. It became something they both loved and added a new dimension to their already strong relationship.

"Later, when I was back in Georgia for a few days, I took a nature walk with Grandmother," Rachel recalls. "We were walking around the grounds at the Chick-fil-A office, and Grandmother turned to me and said, 'Rachel, you're ready.' I was like, 'What do you mean I'm ready? Ready for what?' Grandmother said, 'Next time you're in Georgia, I want you to come over to the house and have a painting day with me.'"

So, the next time Rachel was in town on business, she stayed an extra day to spend with Mom. My mother was so excited about that trip and went out of her way to make sure it was extra special. She made a few shopping trips to the art store and recruited Dad's assistant to help her find a copy of her favorite art book, which had gone out of print years earlier. She was ready to burst with excitement by the day Rachel was scheduled to visit.

Rachel remembers, "When I got to her house, Grandmother was all smiles. We sat on the couch and talked for a few minutes, and then she went over to the cabinet and pulled out a huge shopping bag. She brought it over to me and pulled out three canvases, some paint, and some brushes. I was just shocked. I was floored that she had thought of me and that she had gotten all these things to make the day extra special. And then she gave me an old copy of her favorite book on oil painting that had really helped her grow as an artist, and I couldn't get over it. I mean, if the day had ended then and there, it still would have been a special memory. But there was still so much more.

"Next," Rachel continues, "we went back to her little studio. It was full of life and light. The walls were filled with some of the paintings she'd created, and you could see natural light and the beauty of the farm pouring in through the windows. I love that room. We sat down in there and she helped me get my canvas ready. Then, she said, 'Okay, Rachel, it's time to mix our oils.' I was a little embarrassed and said, 'Um, Grandmother, I don't know what you mean. You'll have to teach me.' She just smiled at me and came over to my seat and walked me through how to squeeze the oils out onto the palette and mix it up with other colors. We spent the rest of the day painting and talking together.

"It just made my heart sing that she would be willing to spend the day with me and teach me these things that she had learned and taught herself. It felt like she was giving me a special piece of herself, and it made my heart happy. I'll never forget that day as long as I live."

Mom never forgot it either. She loved sharing that piece of her heart with her grandchildren, just as she shared her love of music with Dan, Bubba, and me. It was a way for her to pour life into those she loved, to give them a gift that would enrich their lives for years to come.

And it certainly has.

CHAPTER 20

The First Lady of Chick-fil-A

M y brother Dan, who now serves as the Chairman and CEO of Chick-fil-A, often refers to my mother as "the First Lady of Chick-fil-A." I love that title. After reading so many stories about Mom's early life and her years raising us on the farm, you might think she stayed out of the business affairs completely. While it's true she didn't meddle in the day-to-day work of the company, her influence can still be felt on every part of the organization, from each of our local restaurants to each team working in our corporate office in Atlanta. Everyone associated with Chick-fil-A is the beneficiary of Jeannette Cathy's work and heart—and they all know it.

Mom was at Dad's side almost from the beginning. They got married just a few years into his Dwarf Grill business, when he was still running things with his brother and business partner, Ben. She was there when the full weight of the business fell on Dad's shoulders after Ben's death. She did the books, worked the cash register, helped wherever she could, and provided entertainment (in the form of singing children) to customers and staff. Those are the things she did that people could see. For every act of service she did out in the open, though, there were a thousand other things she did outside of public view, when it was just her and my father.

She was his rock, his safe place, his counselor, his coach, his advisor, and his prayer warrior. She sent him out the door with a full heart and completely covered in prayer every morning. She welcomed him home with a kiss and conversation every night—even the nights when he was two hours late or when he brought unexpected dinner guests home with him. She was his sounding board, listening to him talk about the challenges he was facing and always offering perfectly timed and well-prayed-over suggestions. They were partners in every sense of the word—marriage partners, parenting partners, prayer partners, life partners, and business partners. As a result, her fingerprints were all over the company. Dad himself never grew tired of saying that Chick-fil-A wouldn't be what it is today if it weren't for my mother. "She can do and has done anything and everything," he'd say. "All I ever did was put a piece of chicken between a buttered bun."

My parents' longtime friend and neighbor, David Akin, jokes about it this way: "Behind every successful man is a *surprised* woman." I don't know how "surprised" Mom was about Dad's success, but I also don't know how successful he would have been without her supporting him. That was her role and her greatest contribution to the business: support. She was a brilliant woman and really could have done anything she wanted to, but she knew full well why God put her on this earth. She was there to support other people—specifically, her husband, her children, and her ever-expanding Chick-fil-A family. As long as she was doing that, she knew she was being successful in life and a good steward of the opportunities and resources God had given her.

Too many people in the world turn their noses down at those in support roles. Not my mother. Mom knew the weight of the world rests on the shoulders of those who can support it. Without them, everything would come crashing down. That commitment to service and support fills every crack and crevice of our family's business. It's why our team members respond to any request with a heartfelt "My pleasure." They're echoing the heart of my mother, who really did take pleasure in serving other people. Nothing pleased her more than finding a special, unique way to meet another person's need in a very personal way.

Mom's commitment to supporting others is evident in the very name of the Chick-fil-A corporate office. For many years, we called it the "Corporate Office" or "Home Office," but those boring old names never really reflected the heart of the organization. Shortly after Mom's death, the name was changed to the Chick-fil-A Support Center. We know, just as my mother knew, that everyone in that building is there for one and only one reason: to support the thousands of Operators and team members out in the field in our local restaurants. Chick-fil-A doesn't exist for the people working inside the walls of our mothership campus. Rather, we exist to fulfill our mission statement: "To glorify God by being a faithful steward of all that is entrusted to us and to have a positive influence on all who come into contact with Chick-fil-A." Those of us who work out of the Support Center achieve that mission by *supporting* those in the field. That came straight from my mother. In a sense, our home was the very first Chick-fil-A Support Center. That's where she supported Dad.

It's also for this reason that we instituted the highest award a staff member in the Support Center can win, rightly named the Jeannette Cathy Service Award. This award goes to the person in the Support Center who most demonstrates a servant's heart by supporting the Operators across the country. Everyone in the organization knows we aren't winning if we aren't serving—a lesson my mother taught all of us in every interaction.

As Chick-fil-A's first spouse, Mom took a special interest in the wives and husbands of our Operators across the country. She knew better than anyone how many hours and how much effort it took for a restaurant owner to get a business up and running, and she knew the toll it could take on the operator's family. So whenever she attended Chick-fil-A events, she always focused on the spouses. She was sure to spend time with them and to encourage them in their role, making sure they knew how much Chick-fil-A appreciated *their* role in the business.

This became such a passion for her that she eventually made up a special gift for the spouses *behind* the men and women of Chick-fil-A. Knowing how important her own unique Chick-fil-A pin was to her, Mom worked with a designer to create a special "Eat Mor Chikin" Chick-fil-A logo pin. She had a huge batch of these made and always had a handful in her purse or pocket at business functions. Whenever she talked to the spouse of an Operator she reached into her bag and said, "I have a special gift just for you. I know how much you've sacrificed for this company, and I want you to know how much we all appreciate you." Then she'd hand them their very own, unique, can't-get-it-anywhere-else cow pin. It was a simple token of appreciation, but it became a prized possession as word spread among the Operators It meant the world to them to know that the founder's wife was leading the charge to show support and encouragement to their spouses.

One of the most incredible things Mom ever did for Chick-fil-A was to ask a simple question, "What if we got rid of all this debt?" Chick-fil-A has always been intensely focused on financial responsibility—something that flowed from my parents' Depression-era mind-set—but we still use lines of credit to facilitate business operations. One day, my mother was looking over some business documents and wondered aloud why we were carrying so much debt. She talked it over with Dad, and they discussed it further with the company leadership. As a result of her daring to ask the question, Chick-fil-A began a decade-long campaign to become debt-free. It took a while, but Chick-fil-A finally hit the debt-free mark and we all celebrated the accomplishment. While the company still uses lines of credit today and we haven't made debt-freedom a corporate value, it was a powerful lesson to all of us in the value of setting big goals and following through with them. It also showed us that we were perfectly capable of doing something as a business that most people assume couldn't be done: run a multibillion-dollar company with no debt. We *thought* it was possible, but now we *know* . . . because my mother challenged us to figure it out.

Mom never made a big deal of it, but her influence was evident throughout the business's growth in big and small ways, right down to identifying new markets for Chick-fil-A expansion. Her presence was always felt in board rooms, conversations, and business decisions at every level—especially the decisions my dad was personally involved in.

She made quite an impact considering the fact that she was rarely seen at the office. After Dad died, though, Mom surprised us a bit with how concerned she suddenly became about the business and our employees. She knew every single staff member represented a family that depended on Chick-fil-A for their income. Even though Dad had been unplugged from the nitty-gritty details of the business's day-to-day operations for more than a year at that point, Mom felt the weight of the owner's responsibility when he was gone. Just after Thanksgiving 2014, a few months after Dad's passing, Mom had a conversation with Dan that reminded us just how much she cared for every member of our Chick-fil-A family. On one of his visits, she said, "Now, Dan, Christmas is coming up. I know we've always given bonuses to our staff, and I know your father always reviewed the list of bonuses before they went out. He's gone now, and no one has sent me the list to review. I want to make sure you're still giving those bonuses to those families, so let me know if I need to review it."

Dan was himself in his sixties by this point, and he'd presided over Chick-fil-A for several years. Of course, he and his leadership team had taken care of the Christmas bonuses. He just smiled, patted her hand, and said, "Yes, ma'am. We've taken care of it. You don't have to worry about that." It was such a sweet reminder of her heart for the team members who'd become part of our family. She was just as concerned about the thousands of employees we had at that time as she had been about the dozen employees they had at the Dwarf Grill sixty-five years earlier. It didn't matter how many (or how few) people there were; she needed to know that every one of them was being cared for.

As comfortable as she was singing and dancing on stage for most of her life, Mom never liked to get in front of a crowd just to talk. Public speaking made her nervous. You can hear it in her voice if you were to listen to or watch a recording of one of her rare speaking engagements. I think the obvious nerves in her shaky voice made her teaching and testimonies even more powerful. I actually heard her tell a crowd at a women's ministry event, "I don't know how in the world I got the privilege of speaking to you all today, but here we are." The crowd loved it, not because she was being sarcastic but because she genuinely didn't see herself as anything special. She had no idea how much of a powerful and inspiring force she really was. Many speakers will tell a crowd how honored they are to speak to them, but my mother *really* meant it. She was always surprised when someone asked her to speak, and she always took each engagement seriously. I have page after page of her speech drafts, some typed, some handwritten, and some with both typed notes *and* handwritten, last-minute corrections and additions. My mother never "phoned it in" for any group, and that was doubly true for any Chick-fil-A speaking requests. She always felt everyone, especially her Chick-fil-A family, deserved the very best she had to offer—even if she didn't *think* she had much to offer at all.

Despite all her awards and accolades, Mom remained incredibly humble to the very end. She wore her success lightly, never once using it to gain an advantage, manipulate another person, or exert undue influence on anyone. Rather, she approached everyone she encountered with a heart of humility. Whether it was an executive at Chick-fil-A or the young lady scanning her groceries at the supermarket, Mom was overwhelmingly concerned with the needs of the people around her.

She was, in every way, a servant, and it's a blessing to see her life and legacy live on through the kind hearts and acts of service I see in our Chick-fil-A team members every day. Every one of them reflects her passion for service . . . even if they don't realize it.

CHAPTER 21

The Spiritual Nucleus of Our Family

My Granny, Mom's mother, was an amazing woman. She was a hero, in fact. When her husband walked out on her and three-month-old Jeannette, Granny somehow created a life for her little family. She gave my mother a wonderful, rich home life. She introduced my mother to the arts and supported her as she expressed interest in singing and dancing. She worked days creating costumes for dancing schools and the Fox Theatre and she worked nights making sure the Fox performers' costumes stayed in tip-top shape throughout their stage shows. Granny shouldered the burden of single parenthood during the Great Depression, taking care of her daughter while also helping support her parents. She was a fierce powerhouse of self-reliance, and she passed that passion for personal responsibility and self-sufficiency to my mother. My grandmother gave my mother—and, through her, my brothers and me—so many wonderful gifts. She was truly a remarkable woman.

As hard as Granny worked to provide a stable home life for my mother, there were two things Granny simply didn't have to give. First, Granny's hard work and loving hand could not make up for the lack of a strong father figure. I know there are millions of single mothers working unbelievably hard to provide for their sons and daughters around the world today. You may be a hard-working single mother yourself, so please do not misunderstand me. I'm certainly not saying single mothers are doomed to fail simply because there isn't a man around. Far from it! Granny did an incredible job raising my mother, and she did it all on her own. However, her love and attention still could not overcome the absence my mother felt in her heart. Even at an early age, Mom felt something missing. She knew she needed and desperately wanted some kind of father.

Second, Granny couldn't offer my mother a strong spiritual identity. She'd been raised outside of church and did not have a personal relationship with the Lord when Mom was born. Her family rarely went to church and neither Granny nor her parents read or talked about the Bible much at all when my mother was young. The whole concept of God was almost foreign to my mother for the first five years of her life.

I think it was these two things—the absence of a father and the spiritual void in her life—that made the idea of a heavenly Father who loved her and wanted a relationship with her such a revelation to my mother when she first heard about the Lord. She was only five years old when some neighbor friends invited her to go to church with them. The atmosphere was strange to her and, like any child, she thought the phrase

Sunday School was an oxymoron. *School on Sunday?* she must have thought. *I don't know about this.* However, she happily went and enjoyed the games she played and songs she sang at church. It was the mention of a heavenly Father that really got her attention, though. She was so excited to hear that she really *did* have a father. Not just any father, but a perfect, almighty, all-loving, and ever-present Father. Most importantly, a Father who would never leave her. Even at such a young age, her spirit lit up at the news. She couldn't wait to run home and tell her mother all about her new Father.

I imagine Granny was skeptical at first. Who wouldn't be skeptical of the Gospel message filtered through a five-year-old's imagination and exuberance? To her credit, though, Granny listened. She *really* listened and, miraculously, she believed too. With humility, she allowed her young daughter to lead her into a saving relationship with Jesus Christ. The pair were later baptized together, dedicating their lives to the Lord as mother and child. Knowing what it's like to have daughters of my own, this whole scene chokes me up. I can't imagine a more special or intimate experience for a mother to share with her little girl.

From there, as I've said before, Mom dedicated her time and her life to her Father's service. She traveled with missionaries, played piano in church, gave up dancing in front of "secular" crowds in favor of singing for the Lord on weekends, and eventually went to college and seminary. She always thought she'd marry one of the pastors she went to school with and join him in his ministry. Imagine her surprise, then, when she "married a chicken man," as she often joked. She never could have guessed how many ministry opportunities she'd have serving side-by-side with her "chicken man."

Chief among those opportunities was creating a Christ-honoring home and raising three children who love the Lord. I was blessed with two parents who dedicated their lives to Him, and I would never diminish my father's faith. He was bold in his beliefs, strong in his convictions, and unapologetic in his faith, yet he always managed to demonstrate humility and compassion in the way he expressed his commitment to Jesus. It was an incredible mix—certainly among America's leading entrepreneurs. That said, my brothers and I always saw our mother as the spiritual center of our family.

Maybe it was simply because we spent so much more time with her, day in and day out, learning Scripture, serving in church, playing worship music on our instruments, and singing praise songs. We were always around to hear her ongoing conversations with her heavenly Father. We saw her live out her faith in every moment, every day. We watched as she depended wholly on Him to get her out of the taxing, troubling, and often hilarious problems she had on the farm. We witnessed the countless hours she spent at her little glass kitchen table studying her Bible and Sunday School materials. We heard the preachers' voices from the radio and television echoing through the house. To grow up in the Cathy home was to grow up fully immersed in the Spirit of God. It filled my mother and overflowed onto the rest of us. It was impossible to be around her—especially to be with her every day—without getting drenched in the faith that poured out of her. That's why my brother Dan once called my mother the *spiritual nucleus* of our family. We each had our own active relationship with the Lord, but our mother's faith was home base for the Cathy family. She's the one who really showed us what it meant to love God and honor Him with our lives.

One of the most impressive things about Mom's faith was her commitment to Bible study. It was rare to see her study with *just* the Bible. She usually had one or two commentaries on the table next to her Bible in addition to a notepad, index card, or scrap of paper for writing notes. Oh, those notes! To this day, her home is filled with sermon notes, spiritual reflections, prayers, application principles from different Bible passages, and other random spiritual musings. We found them laying on tables, taped to mirrors, stuffed in books, sitting on the piano bench, stuck on the refrigerator, and jammed into every other nook and cranny throughout the house. You couldn't walk from the kitchen to a bedroom without seeing at least three mini-sermons and five biblical Greek word studies! Taking a tour of her home was and still is a discipleship journey; there's a good chance someone could come into a saving relationship with Jesus and mature in their faith between the front door and back door of the farmhouse! Those little notes say so much about who Jeannette Cathy was; I just couldn't bear to remove them after she died.

Her seminary-honed knack for Bible study didn't stop with what she wrote on paper, though. She also committed to writing the Word on her heart and mind. Mom was relentless in Scripture memorization. She drilled that into us as children—we always had to work on memory verses each week—but we could never complain that she was making us do something she wasn't doing herself. She wasn't simply memorizing verses or small passages, either; she memorized entire chapters and books of the Bible. I've still never seen anything like it. I remember one time when Dan came in all excited to tell Mom he'd memorized the entire seventh chapter of Matthew's Gospel. He was married and probably a parent himself by this point, but he was still proud to come recite the passage for our mother.

Dan recalls, "We sat down at the table together, and I recited Matthew 7 perfectly. I felt pretty good about myself at that point. Mom looked at me and said, 'Honey, that is so good. Great job! Now, of course you know the seventh chapter of Matthew is really the end of a three-chapter block made up of chapters five, six, and seven. Here, let me tell you what chapters five and six say.' Then, purely from memory and with no preparation, Mom perfectly recited the other two chapters for me. To be honest, she really put me in my place that morning."

Bubba has fond memories of our mother's Bible study too. One of the great treasures of his life is the Bible our parents gave him on his sixteenth birthday. On the dedication page, Mom wrote him a simple note that forever shaped his approach to Bible study (and making time for Bible study). It reads, "Bubba, sin will keep you from this Book, and this Book will keep you from sin. With love, Mom and Dad, 1970." So true. It's been fifty years since they gave Bubba that gift, and he's seen that note nearly every day since. I love that Mom is still there, encouraging him in his Bible study.

My mother was just as known for her rich prayer life as she was her intense Bible study. Since she viewed prayer as an ongoing conversation with her Father, I doubt she ever prayed the same prayer the same way twice. She didn't focus on flowery language and never once gave the impression that she was trying to *impress* God with the way she spoke. Rather, she just talked to Him. Sure, her words were full of passion and power, but, at the heart of it, she was simply talking to her Father. Mom never rushed through her prayers, either. She knew there was nothing more important than the time she spent with Him, so she never tried to hurry their conversations along the way you might try to rush through a phone call with a friend. When it came to her one-on-one chats with her Father, she had all the time in the world.

My parents' farmhand Chris spent several minutes almost every day waiting on Mom and Dad to finish their morning prayers before he entered the house. He recently told me, "I brought them their newspaper every morning when I got to the farm, and I'd have to wait on them to finish their prayers before I walked in. I never wanted to interrupt them because they were so focused on what they were praying. And Mrs. Jeannette would just pray and pray for anything and everything. They'd say a long prayer every morning, covering everything from the rocks to the sky. It was so humbling to hear them, to get that picture of their faith. I'd just stand outside the kitchen door and watch them pray for ten minutes or more, pouring their hearts out for pretty much everyone—well, everyone but themselves, that is. They spent so much time praying for other people by name, it was like they never thought to stop and pray for themselves."

Dad's longtime executive assistant, Martha Lawrence, often got a front-row seat to their morning prayer routine too. As Dad got older and stopped driving, Martha would occasionally swing by the house to pick Dad up and drive him to the office. When I asked her about it recently, she said, "When I got there to pick him up, I'd see them sitting at the kitchen table together. Nine times out of ten, her Bible would be open next to her Sunday School book. You could tell they were either in the middle of a morning devotion or had just finished it. And then they'd always pray together. Jeannette took prayer so seriously. If I ever mentioned something going on in my family, she'd always say she'd pray about it—and I knew she would, because she'd follow up on it sometime later. When she'd ask how specific things were going weeks after we talked about it, I'd think, *Wow, she really is keeping this top of mind in her prayers.* Being able to pray for someone else was very special to her. She saw it as an honor and privilege that she took seriously."

Martha said something else that really paints a picture of my mother's life of faith: "Jeannette's faith was just a mainstay of her life; it was part of who she was, and she didn't apologize for it or try to hide it. She woke up and put her faith on just like her clothes, there for all the world to see." I can't think of a better way to describe my mother's faith. She really did put it on every morning; it was as obvious and clear as the clothes on her back to everyone around her. From the age of five until her death at ninety-two, it was impossible to see Jeannette McNeil Cathy without seeing her heavenly Father right there beside her.

Truly, I have never seen anyone as fiercely committed in their faith, as passionate about prayer and Bible study, and as humble in exercising the power of their spirit as my mother. I doubt I ever will.

CHAPTER 22

When Mom Erases the Faces

*S*teve Penley is one of the most celebrated artists working today. He's been praised far and wide for his bold use of colors, large brushstrokes, and unmistakable style. He's particularly wellknown for his political paintings, capturing the likenesses of George Washington, Ronald Reagan, Hillary Clinton, John F. Kennedy, Abraham Lincoln, Winston Churchill, and many others in his trademark style. His bold interpretations of the American flag, the Statue of Liberty, Mount Rushmore, and Washington crossing the Delaware have made him a favorite among modern American politicians. In fact, his work adorns the offices of dozens of U.S. Congresspeople and senators throughout Washington, D.C. He is truly a master of his craft in every sense of the word. And my mother smeared white paint all over one of his most precious works of art.

As Chick-fil-A neared the fortieth anniversary of its first mall location, someone in the organization came up with a fabulous idea. What better way to memorialize such a landmark achievement than to have the world-famous Steve Penley create a new piece representing his unique vision of Chick-fil-A's history? Everyone involved got excited, but they didn't tell my parents. The goal wasn't just to create something we could hang in the office; rather, this was meant to be a cherished gift to Dad and Mom, something they could treasure in honor of their lifelong commitment to building Chick-fil-A into what it had become. Of course, I'm sure whoever came up with the idea hoped they would offer to lend the painting back to Chick-fil-A, possibly to hang in our Support Center in Atlanta or maybe even display in the original Dwarf House among the old photographs posted on the wall.

Chick-fil-A reached out to Steve to put the plan in motion. Living and working in Atlanta, Steve Penley was certainly no stranger to Chick-fil-A. He had long invested much of his time in local endeavors and businesses. In fact, he's nearly as famous for his paintings of Coca-Cola as he is for his political work. He sees Coke as an expression of Americana, and he must have painted dozens of Coke-themed creations over the years. After talking to our team, he was thrilled to lend his talents to another popular Atlanta-based business, Chick-fil-A.

His goal was simple: create an artistic history of Chick-fil-A and Truett Cathy to celebrate forty years of operating under the Chick-fil-A name. The team gave him a few photographs as inspiration and sat with him to tell him some key stories from the company's history. With that, Penley went to work and created a magnificent portrait. Everyone who saw it was thrilled with how it turned out. It beautifully captured a few key scenes from Chick-fil-A's proud history. Prominently displayed at the top was a large image of Dad's smiling face next to our iconic Chick-fil-A cows and their "Eat Mor Chikin" signs. At the bottom was the Chick-fil-A logo with a fortieth anniversary banner and a perfect rendition of Dad's original Dwarf Grill, where Chick-fil-A was born. In the middle of the large canvas, there was a picture of Dad on a park bench with a few children, signifying his lifelong commitment to foster children. Next to that was Steve's reimagining of one of my favorite photos of my parents: a picture of them in their early eighties cuddled up together sharing a milkshake from a single Chick-fil-A cup with two straws. At the bottom was the artist's trademark block-lettered signature, PENLEY.

The painting was, in a word, perfect. It presented the history of the company, the heart of my parents, and a celebration of forty successful years through Penley's unmistakably unique artistic vision. Plans were made to unveil the masterpiece to my parents, and everyone involved saw it as a grand success. They never could have guessed what would happen next.

When the day of the big reveal came, things did not go as the organizers planned. Dad, of course, loved the painting. He went on and on about how personal and unique it was, and he especially loved to see the inclusion of foster children, representing his commitment to WinShape Homes, the foster-care program he and Mom established through the WinShape Foundation. No history of his life—even in a painting—would be complete without at least *some* representation of his love for children and the good work WinShape Homes had done over the years. And, of course, he loved seeing his wife memorialized along with him as part of Chick-fil-A's history. He knew none of it would have been possible without her, and he especially loved that picture of the two of them. The smile on his face went ear to ear.

The gift was a big win—at least as far as Dad was concerned. There was only one problem: my mother hated it. Well, *hate* may be too strong a word. I think the big issue was that she wasn't familiar with Penley's work, so she wasn't prepared for his unique style, especially when it came to how he paints faces. My mother had been painting for twenty years by this point, so she had settled into a particular artistic style of her own. She tended to paint more realistic interpretations of faces. As I said earlier, the painting of the woman that hangs above Mom's piano almost looks like a photograph. The skin tones, the lines on her face, and especially her eyes—it all looks photorealistic. Penley, however, has a much different style. This was clearly a case of clashing artistic visions, and my mother simply didn't *get it*.

She thought the cows were pretty good, and she was fine with the anniversary logo and the image of the Dwarf Grill. She was even okay with the large picture of Dad's face at the top and how Penley represented the foster children from WinShape Homes. What she could not get past, though, was his interpretation of the classic "Truett and Jeannette milkshake-sharing picture." That's a photo she was intimately familiar with; she'd looked at it hundreds of times and knew every curve, line, shadow, and wrinkle. And let's not ignore the fact that it was the only picture of *her* on the canvas. *Of course,* her eyes went straight to it—*any* woman's eyes would go straight to it!

Reviewing the picture with Dad, Mom said, "No. No, this won't do. It doesn't even look like us!" With that, any hopes the Chick-fil-A organizers had of hanging that picture in the office or at the Dwarf House went up in smoke.

Here's where the story took a weird, unexpected turn. My mother, dedicated artist that she was, declared, "I think I can fix it!" Never mind the fact that it was the perfect representation from an iconic painter. Never mind the fact that Chick-fil-A had spent a lot of money commissioning a Penley original. Oh, no. Move over Steve Penley; here comes Jeannette Cathy!

She had the painting moved to the farm. I think she did this for two reasons. First, she had plans for the picture, which I'll get to. Second, I think she didn't want anyone else to see it. There was something about how she looked on that canvas that disturbed her. I'd never seen her react to something quite like that. In her mind, it was one step above a cheap caricature you might have done by a first-year art student at the state fair. My apologies to Steve Penley (but I'm pretty sure he already knows how Mom felt about it).

Soon after, Mom followed through on her threat—err, I mean her *promise*—to try to fix the painting. She got out her brushes and oils, and she painted over her and Dad's faces in the milk-shake-sipping scene. I'm not saying she tweaked them or tried to improve them; I mean she literally *painted over* the faces in white. It was the artistic equivalent of blotting out a little typo with a gallon of Wite-Out. She covered up every inch of their faces with the odd exception of her eyes and lips and one of Dad's ears. I guess she thought Penley's work wasn't a *total* loss. I mean, why repaint an ear if you don't have to?

With the offending faces forever destroyed by the world's sweetest, most grandmotherly art vandal, she stopped. That's it. That's all she wanted to do. Whether or not she planned on *ever* repainting the faces is a mystery. Apparently, all she wanted to do was erase them from existence. With that, she was content to set the painting aside for good, condemning it to years in art jail for its crimes against her face.

Like a missing Monet lost to the ravages of time, the infamous Penley Chick-fil-A painting wasn't seen for years afterward. A legend actually began to pop up around it, with Chick-fil-A employees passing the story on to new team members. It was as though my mother had a map to the mythical city of Atlantis locked away in her basement. Everyone was curious about it, but nobody ever saw it. Then, after Dad died in 2014, I helped Mom go through his things and found the painting in their basement.

My daughter Angela and her husband, Brent, were in the process of opening their first Chick-fil-A restaurant in Birmingham, Alabama, around that time. Angela, knowing the full, funny story about the painting, said, "You know, if there's one thing we'd love to have, it's that Penley painting. We'd love to hang it in Brent's store." She told me later she was half-joking, assuming the piece would be too big to bother with or that my mother wouldn't want to bring it back out into the light of day.

I asked Mom about it, and she said, "Well, I don't know *who* would ever want that thing, and I never got around to fixing it. It's going to need some work. But they're welcome to have it if they want it."

Angela and Brent were thrilled, but they still faced a daunting task: taking the ruined picture back to Steve Penley to explain why part of his great painting was whited out. Steve took the whole thing in good humor (as much as he could, anyway), and he graciously agreed to paint Mom and Dad's milkshake-sipping image—*again*—on top of Mom's blob of whitewashed embarrassment. "I'll fix it for you, no problem," he said. "But only under one condition: Jeannette cannot *touch* this painting again!"

It was a deal. In fact, Mom never wanted to see that "awful" painting again. Steve did a wonderful job repainting the sweet scene of my parents sharing a milkshake on the canvas. If you didn't know the full story, you'd never guess that part of the painting was several years newer than the rest of it! With the magnificent Penley original freshly restored once and for all, Brent and Angela proudly hung the fortieth anniversary painting in their new restaurant—eight years *after* Chick-fil-A's fortieth anniversary. You can see it there today, prominently displayed in Chick-fil-A Greystone in Birmingham.

Sadly, Mom never saw it hanging in all its glory as it was intended: in a Chick-fil-A restaurant for all our customers to enjoy. She died soon after, leaving Angela with a gift that's come to symbolize so many great things about her grandmother: her spirit, her spunk, her artistry, and, of course, her gallons and gallons of spare white paint.

CHAPTER 23

Hidden Treasures

For about fifteen years—from age sixty-five to eighty—Mom painted nearly every day. It became one of her greatest passions. She couldn't imagine what her life would look like if she wasn't able to get back to her little studio and pour her heart and soul onto a canvas. It didn't take her long to fill her house up with her artwork. Every wall in every room was a testament to her artistic genius. Landscapes, portraits, farm scenes, still life, fruit, animals—she painted it all. She painted for herself, she painted gifts for others, she painted by request, and, most importantly, she painted as an act of worship. God had given her an amazing capacity to see His Creation through His eyes, and she rejoiced at finally having a way to express all the beauty she saw in the world. And through her art, the rest of us got a glimpse of *what* she saw and *how* she saw it. It was truly an amazing gift, and it's one we're so grateful she shared with us.

Sometime around age eighty, though, she started slowing down. She'd had some health problems that had taken a toll on her, and her painting dwindled until she finally quit altogether. I don't think she ever made the conscious decision to stop painting; I just think it gradually slowed to a standstill. That began an entire decade of no new paintings. This was quite a loss for those of us who loved seeing her heart through her work. As the constant flow of new art dried up, we all began to realize how much we missed seeing new pieces. It was like an important, vibrant piece of my mother just disappeared—and we all wanted it back.

Fortunately for us, her cardiologist wanted it back too. As Mom entered her nineties, her longtime friend and doctor, Dr. Charles Wilmer, encouraged her to get back into painting. He knew it would not only keep her mind sharp but it would also help maintain her fine motor skills, both of which are crucial for people at that age. Surprisingly, Mom resisted her doctor's orders to start painting again. After some time, though, she did try to take it up again, but it felt more difficult than she'd ever known it. Her skills weren't what they once were, and she knew it. She knew what to look for and what to critique, and she realized the ten years of inactivity had taken a toll. Because the doctor had made such a big deal of it, though, I wouldn't let Mom off the hook. John and I had returned to Georgia from Virginia by then, and we built our house on the property near Mom and Dad's farmhouse. That meant, for the first time in decades, I was able to see Mom every day. It *also* meant that I was in the perfect position to nag Mom into following her doctor's advice!

I signed her up for art classes at the local art store to get the old juices flowing again. Little by little, she got more comfortable and her confidence returned. Her hand wasn't quite as steady as it had been a decade earlier, but she worked through it. This began a renaissance of Jeannette Cathy originals. She wasn't nearly as prolific as she'd been during the busy years, but she put even more love and care into each new piece she painted. The projects she selected were more personal than ever. She still did nature scenes, of course, but her main focus was on the people around her—her grandchildren and great-grandchildren. She knew she was in the final years of her life, so she viewed her art through more of a legacy lens. She didn't have time to paint *everyone*, but she was determined to use her remaining years to paint things that really mattered for those she'd soon leave behind.

One of our family favorites, in fact, was a beautiful portrait of her great-granddaughter Reese. Mom came across a photo my son John sent her years earlier of his then three-year-old daughter holding two dead leaves in the air. Reese had the most captivating smile on her face as she reached up to her parents with a leaf in each hand, as though she'd found a priceless treasure and couldn't wait to show it off. Her little golden pigtails shot out of each side of her head in a picture that screamed, "Look at me, Mommy! Look what I found!" It was honestly one of the most adorable photographs I've ever seen in my life. When Mom rediscovered that picture, she couldn't help but be captivated by its beauty. While she was feeling the aches and pains of old age, here was a picture that celebrated the light and life of youth. She knew immediately that she simply *had* to paint it.

Mom went to work capturing the scene onto her canvas. She sketched it lightly in pencil, taking great pains to get every line and nuance of Reese's little face just right. She chose brighter colors than what was shown in the photo, again capturing *how she saw the world* instead of how it actually was. And, of course, it just wouldn't do to have two old, dead leaves in this piece of art. So, she replaced those leaves with daffodils, giving the little darling two perfect flowers to lift high into the air. When she was finished, we were all amazed at what we saw. You can feel the love exploding off the canvas. As far as we were concerned, this was a perfect painting, something our family will treasure forever.

This wasn't just one of Mom's *best* paintings; it was the last one she ever completed. That's fitting in a way, as Reese *McNeil* White was partially named after my mother. Reese's portrait is still sitting on the easel in Mom's studio just where she left it. I'm sure it'll go to John or Reese someday, but we couldn't bear to move it after Mom died. When I walk into the studio even today, it's as though the paint is still wet on the canvas, like Mom just stepped out of the room to clean her brushes and wash her hands and will be back at any second.

Sometimes, when I'm feeling lonely for my mother or disconnected from her by the years since her passing, I stand in that little studio that was once my childhood bedroom. From that one spot, I can feel a lifetime of moments with her. I can see her sitting on the side of my bed praying with me at bedtime. I can hear her words of wisdom when I was struggling with the heartache and heartbreak of teen angst. I can feel the spirit pouring out of her as she offers her gift of painting to the Lord in an act of worship. I can hear her chatting away with her heavenly Father as they toil together on a timeless work of art. She's been gone for several years now, but her sweet spirit still fills that room.

After years of so many gifts and wonders coming out of that studio, we were all surprised to find one of her most precious gifts hiding in the closet after she died. After the funeral, I was going through her things in the house, deciding what to do with everything she and Dad had left behind. While rummaging around in her studio, I found a canvas tucked away in the closet that none of us had ever seen before. I pulled it out and was stunned by what

I saw. While the beautiful portrait of Reese was the last painting Mom *completed*, it may not have been the last one she worked on. She left one unfinished and hidden away from the world. Centered on the canvas was a face Mom and I both knew and loved. The bald head, big, brown eyes, loving smile, and slightly oversized ears of my father beamed off the canvas. That face—mostly complete—is the only part of the portrait Mom finished. It's surrounded by the canvas's untouched field of white with only light pencil sketches outlining Dad's shoulders, suit, and tie.

I can't tell you how special it is to our family to know that this may have been the last painting Mom was working on before she died. To know that she was offering everything she had to the love of her life even to the very end means everything to us. It is the perfect representation of their marriage. Always *for* each other, always *with* each other. Even death couldn't break that bond. Of all the incredible pieces Mom painted over the years, that one—that unfinished, half-realized portrait of my father—might be my favorite one. It's the lost treasure Mom left for us to find, and it's worth is beyond measure to those of us who knew and loved them both so much.

CHAPTER 24

With Love, Grandmother

If you were to walk through Mom and Dad's farm-house today, you'd notice three things throughout the house. First, you'd see Mom's paintings, and second, you'd see her handwritten notes throughout the house. She left sermon notes and Bible study thoughts at her spot at the kitchen table and in her little makeshift study, and she left helpful reminders to herself here and there. If she had recently rearranged the cabinets, for example, she'd leave a note in one cabinet that said something like, "Coffee cups now to the left of the fridge." And, next to the whole-home audio system that was installed in the 1980s, she wrote labels for which button does what. She was a brilliant woman, but even she needed some help remembering these kinds of things.

Third (and most importantly), you'd see pictures of her family. And you'd see them *everywhere*. Every wall, table, counter, shelf, and any other surface has at least one or two photographs of her family. Walking down the narrow hall to her bedroom, in fact, can be a little tricky. She crammed as many pictures as possible of all sizes on both sides of the hall walls. On one side, she has pictures devoted to her three children. Dan, Bubba, and I each have a dedicated section of wall with pictures of our childhood, graduations, spouses, weddings, and every special event you could think of. She even has our old business cards pressed into the frames here and there to add a little Chick-fil-A flavor to the literal walk through our lives.

On the facing wall are pictures of her grandchildren and great-grandchildren. This is where things *really* seem crowded. My parents had twelve grandchildren and lived long enough to see most of those twelve grow up to start families of their own. Mom had twenty great-grandchildren at the time of her death (it's up to twenty-nine today), and she had a personal relationship with each one. She absolutely *had* to have pictures of every one of them in the Cathy Gallery up and down the hallway. Space was so tight on that particular wall that she could only use small pictures, mostly wallet size, in tiny frames. She had several narrow shelves installed on the wall so each grandchild's family could have a few inches of dedicated space, and she organized those pictures perfectly in the world's most sentimental game of Tetris.

One of her great-grandchildren, who all called her GG (short for great-grandmother), once asked, "GG, why do you have so many pictures of all of us all over the place?"

Mom just smiled and said, "Oh honey, it's because I always want to remember to pray for each and every one of you whenever I walk by your picture!" None of the grandchildren or great-grands, as Mom called them, ever doubted that she prayed over them by name every day.

My mother was blessed with a special connection to children, something she nurtured through her decades teaching eight-grade Sunday School. She never diminished the concerns of an adolescent girl or laughed off the worries of a young boy. Instead, she showed respect for each child and honored the life each one was living and the decisions they were making. When she asked her grand-children and great-grands what was going on in their lives, they knew she was *really* interested. They also knew she would pray for their concerns with passion, talking to her heavenly Father about whatever the children were going through. More than that, Mom would always follow up with the children weeks—even months—after first discussing a prayer concern with them. She'd ask the girls how dancing or gymnastics was going and ask the boys about the sports they were playing. She remembered the names of their friends and the people they were dating and always asked detailed questions that showed just how much she cared and how much she remembered from one conversation to another. I don't know how she managed to keep up with so much about so many people and things, but she never missed a beat. And her grandchildren and great-grands noticed.

Never settling for the ordinary or bare-minimum grand-motherly attention, Mom always tried to come up with unique ways to show her love to each grandchild. Sometimes, that meant going the extra mile for one child in particular, such as when she threw Joy a polka-dotted chicken pox birthday party. Other times, though, Mom searched for ways to show the whole bunch how much she loved them *and* loved being their grandmother. That's the motivation behind one of her most extraordinary ideas and a gift that is still be being given years after her death.

As her grandchildren grew up and started getting married, Mom wanted to do something extra special for all of them. After a lot of thinking and planning, she decided to expand something she and Dad had done for my brothers, sisters-in-law, husband, and me years earlier. One Christmas, Dad had special rings designed for Dan, Bubba, and my husband, John. Years later, at Christmas, Mom had pendant necklaces made for my sisters-in-law, Rhonda and Cindy, and me. Each one was designed very simply with a band of gold containing three small diamonds. Mom had the wonderful idea of having a new batch of rings and necklaces made for each of her grandchildren and their current and future spouses. This would be far more than a simple wedding gift; it would become a hallmark Cathy family legacy piece.

As nice as the pieces were, it was the thought and the meaning behind the gift that made it especially important. The three diamonds represented Mom and Dad's "Three Ms" teaching, reinforcing their focus on master, mate, and mission. My parents were careful to make sure every grandchild heard that teaching a few times throughout their lives. Then, when the grandchild got married, they gave the bride a necklace and the groom a ring along with a personalized note. When my daughter Joy married Trent, for example, their ring and pendant came with this note:

> Jeannette and I are so pleased to have you, Trent, as an addition to our family. You and Joy have made a strong commitment to each other and have indicated this by exchanging rings. Jeannette and I are indeed privileged and honored to present these tokens to you, Trent and Joy, for your remembrance and to reassure you of our love for you for as long as you live. With love forever, Truett and Jeannette

This wonderful gift is something every grandchild knew about and something they each looked forward to, knowing they'd receive it on or around their wedding day.

Sadly, Mom and Dad both passed away before all twelve grandchildren got married, but Mom still planned ahead for that. Long before her death, Mom had the complete set made: twelve necklaces and twelve rings, enough for every grandchild and his or her spouse. She also wrote personalized notes for all the grandchildren that hadn't gotten married yet. As she got older and more concerned about her health, Mom gave the stockpile to me to manage. She continued giving them out as each wedding came and went until her death. Then, I divvied up the remaining gifts between Dan, Bubba, and me to manage for our own children.

I love knowing that there are still some men and women in the Cathy family who haven't received their necklaces or rings yet. That means they still have one more gift in their future from their grandmother, who loved them enough to plan a special wedding gift for them long after she was gone.

My mother loved and shared a personal connection with every family member across three generations, from Dan, her own firstborn, to Maverick, the great-grandson who was born three weeks before her death. Maverick is the son of Mark Cathy, one of Bubba's sons. He's also the last Cathy baby Mom had the chance to meet. Mark brought Maverick to a family dinner at Dan's house on a Sunday evening to meet his sweet GG. We have a picture of Mom holding the little guy on her lap. She has such a precious smile on her face in that photo! You can almost feel her pride in seeing how big and beautiful her family had grown. After dinner that Sunday, Mom started feeling bad. We didn't know at that point—and Mark certainly didn't know when they took that picture of Mom and Maverick—that she'd be gone forever by Wednesday.

The picture of Mom and Maverick is the last picture ever taken of my mother . . . and it could not be more perfect. Seeing her beaming with pride and joy while holding her *twentieth* great-grandchild captures so much about her life. She had so much love to give, and she shared it freely and personally to everyone around her—especially her family. Her love ran four generations deep, down to little Maverick, and I know it'll run far deeper and further than that in the years and generations to come.

CHAPTER 25

Sweethearts Till Sunset

s I've been putting stories together for this book, I've had
the chance to spend a lot of time not only *thinking* about
my mother but also talking to close friends and family
members about her. It's been fascinating getting other people's
perspectives on her. What I've found especially interesting is that,
although I've been trying to get stories just about *her,* very few
people can see her apart from my father. Sure, she had her own
rich, full, and meaningful life, but she was really at her best when
she was loving him. The Lord knew what He was doing when
He put those two together. Like my brother Dan recently said,
"You know, it was really fun to see how Mom and Dad loved each
other." I can only pray my own children say that about John and
me long after we're gone.

What's striking about my parents' relationship is how simple
and pure it was. They weren't flashy people at all. Even after all

their success, they were the same Truett and Jeannette that they'd always been. They never got distracted by the trappings of wealth or the pitfalls so many successful couples fall into. Mom never once had to worry about where Dad was, who he was with, or what he was up to. She didn't have a jealous bone in her body, and she knew exactly who that man was. Dad was the same way. At the core of the relationship was the most beautiful sense of love and devotion I've ever seen. Neither could ever even conceive of hurting or betraying the other.

One of the cornerstones of their marriage for as long as I can remember was their daily breakfast date. They had breakfast together at that little glass kitchen table every single day. No matter what time Dad had to get up or how early he needed to be at work, Mom got up with him and prepared breakfast while he showered and dressed. Sometimes, he'd get to the kitchen to find a hot meal of crispy bacon and eggs; other days, they'd feast on cold cereal. This actually became a bit of a game for them. Mom got in the habit of buying several different types of cereal. Her pantry shelves were lined with cereal boxes of all different types: bran, corn, rice, wheat, clusters, fruit and nut, honey nut, Grape Nuts (what is it with cereal and nuts?), sweetened, unsweetened, puffed, flakes—she had it all. Then, at breakfast, she and Dad would mix and match cereals. They'd invent their own combinations by filling their bowls with a little bit of *this* cereal and a little bit of *that* cereal. My sister-in-law Cindy called them *cereal entrepreneurs*!

After they ate, Mom and Dad would pray together at the breakfast table, asking God to bless their marriage, family, business, foster children, and whatever else was on their minds that day. Then, she'd give him a little kiss and send him out the door with a full belly and a fuller heart. It's amazing how something so small—just sharing a bowl of cereal—can make such a big impact in a marriage, but it certainly did for them. Thinking about that daily commitment challenges me to make sure John and I are always paying attention to the little things that matter most in our relationship.

As much as they enjoyed their time at home together, Mom and Dad also loved taking trips together. I'm not talking about annual, lavish, luxury trips to Europe or high-end resorts at the world's finest destinations. Yes, our family enjoyed some big overseas trips together after my brothers and I all got married, but Mom and Dad mainly enjoyed simple trips to the beach. They just loved getting away together or with friends. One year, some friends introduced them to New Smyrna Beach in Florida. They absolutely fell in love with the area and eventually bought a condo there to make it their go-to getaway. Whenever Dad could get away for a few days, they'd pack up and head down to the beach for some well-deserved time off. Most of the time, they'd take some friends with them. That was Dad, always trying to share great experiences with the people around him.

They also enjoyed going on cruises with other couples every now and then. One year, they went on a cruise with their friends Maurice and Helen Harbin that resulted in one of the best pictures ever taken of my parents. The entertainment for that night called for cruise guests to gather into groups and put on silly skits for the audience. My parents and the Harbins were paired with a few other people and tasked with putting on a "shotgun wedding" skit. Everyone had to dress the part in full wedding gowns, dresses, suits, and ties. There was a catch, though: all the women played the men's roles and the men played the women's roles.

So, there was Jeannette Cathy as the groom, decked out in a white tuxedo with a babyblue bowtie and boutonniere and a realistic black mustache glued to her face, walking down the aisle with Mr. Harbin, who was fully made up and dressed in a white gown with two large balloons filling out his chest. The scene was made even funnier by the "bride's" height difference—Mr. Harbin was about two feet taller than my mother! Dad played the mother of the groom and was outfitted in a flowered dress (with balloon "implants" of his own), and Mrs. Harbin rounded out the cast as the angry father of the bride, complete with her own mustache, bowtie, and, of course, a makeshift shotgun. The photograph of this deranged wedding party is priceless. The whole group has huge smiles on their faces, but there's something special about my mother. Everyone who's seen the picture goes straight to my mother standing in the center, her big toothy smile and sparkling eyes capturing the joy of the moment perfectly.

As much as I loved vacationing with my parents, I was always grateful that they made time for child-free getaways. They knew the health of the family depended on their relationship as husband and wife, and they invested heavily into making their marriage not only rock-steady and secure, but also a lot of fun. They really did act like newlyweds most of the time, something people couldn't help but notice. For example, Mom joined Dad for a big Chick-fil-A national event in Nashville, Tennessee, one year. This was late in their lives; they were probably in their eighties. Dad's team thought it would be funny to sneak into the hotel garage where they parked and decorate their car with streamers and balloons and cans tied to the back bumper. They even wrote "Just Married" across the back windshield, just like you'd see on a young couple's car as they drove away from their wedding ceremony.

When the valet pulled up to the front of the hotel in that car, Mom and Dad burst out laughing. They thought it was great, and they kept all the decorations on the car for the entire weekend.

Everyone in attendance got to see the founder and CEO of Chick-fil-A driving his sweetheart around in a "Just Married" car. It was a true testament to how other people saw them, not to mention how they viewed each other and their marriage. My brothers and I—along with our own spouses and children—are the beneficiaries of that amazing legacy of love.

That said, my mother certainly had her share of frustrating days over the years. That's to be expected in any marriage, of course, but especially in families that have grown a huge, nationwide business. Mom wasn't in the office with Dad every day; she was busy holding down the home front, raising children, and caring for farm animals. Dad never hesitated to say that my mother worked just as hard (if not harder) than he did. And, in the midst of that, she often missed her husband. She got annoyed when he missed one too many dinners and was frustrated when he changed their plans at the last minute. Always the problem-solver, Mom spent time thinking through those periods of frustration and came up with a novel solution: she committed to change her expectations. Simply put, she chose not to have any.

I remember once when she had gotten really frustrated about Dad's long hours at work and was feeling lonely in the house all alone. She and I were in the car together driving to an appointment that week, and she said, "You know, Trudy, I think I've figured out the secret to a happy marriage.

I said, "Oh, please tell me, Mom. I can't wait to hear this!"

She replied, "Well, I've noticed the times I get the most frustrated with your father are the times when he didn't do what I thought he *would* do or *should* do. A lot of the time, the problem isn't *him*; the problem is my expectations. So, I'm going to stop expecting anything and we'll see what happens."

Now, that might sound like she was giving up on him, but that's not what she meant at all. She was learning, even decades into their marriage, that she had the ability to *choose* how she felt at any given time. After all, Dad hadn't broken any promises to her; he just hadn't done what she expected him to do. So, from then on, she stopped expecting anything of him. Seriously, she really did. In fact, long after my chat with her in the car, I was at her house and noticed a little note she left to herself. It read, "Do not expect anything. Don't expect *anything*—regardless." I laughed that she left herself a little reminder of her own rule for a happy marriage. I'm sure there were days when she needed it.

One season when Mom tried especially hard to limit her expectations was the final year of Dad's life. He fought a difficult battle against cancer for a year, something I'll discuss more in the following chapter. He was homebound for most of that year; his days of leaving early for a long workday were far behind him. Mom tried to take each day as it came. Some days would be better than others, and Dad would be able to move around the house and maybe even go outside. Other days were harder, leaving him unable to get out of the hospital bed that had been set up in his bedroom. Even though she loved having Dad at home with her all day for the first time in their long marriage, Mom knew expectations could be her downfall. Expecting the best could have left her even more scared and frustrated on his bad days and expecting the worst could have stolen the joy out of all the time they had left together. She refused to do either. Instead, she greeted each day that year with her arms open wide to opportunities rather than with her mind closed by expectations.

On Dad's better days, he was able to get out of the house and Mom would drive him around the farm in their golf cart. That sounds so simple, but those hours were precious to them. A friend recently told me about seeing them out on the farm one afternoon. She actually lived on the property for a few months during that time. Years earlier, my parents had built a small guest house to offer temporary lodging for traveling missionaries, and my friend stayed there while finishing her graduate work. She told me she was studying at home on a beautiful spring afternoon when she saw my parents through the window driving around in the golf cart. They were a good distance away but still clear enough for my friend to see them.

She said, "I saw them driving around and they pulled up to the swing in front of the pond. Your mom got out of the driver's seat and walked around to help your dad out. I could tell he was having a hard time getting down, but your mother supported him the whole time. He leaned on her as he tried to get out and eventually kind of fell out into her arms.

"Then, they walked arm in arm over to the swing and she helped him sit down. She cuddled up next to him, and they sat out there for a long time chatting as the sun set. I couldn't help but wonder what they were talking about. Then, before it got too dark, I saw her get up, help him off the swing, and patiently get him back in the golf cart to drive him home."

My friend said, "I actually felt guilty for watching them, like I was intruding into a private moment, but I couldn't take my eyes off them. It was so beautiful to see how committed she was to him."

I didn't hear this story until several years after their deaths, but I could immediately picture the scene my friend described. It was easy, because that's how I've always seen my parents—as the ultimate sweethearts stealing tender moments together whenever and however they could. They shared many more days together after this particular sunset, but the picture of them rocking back and forth on that swing is one the most endearing and enduring images I have of them now that they're gone.

My mother loved my father more than anything or anyone else on earth. Everything I know about being a godly wife, friend, and partner to my husband came from watching her. It's a gift I can never repay and one that will echo through countless generations of our family for years to come.

CHAPTER 26

*To God Be the
Glory, Great Things
He Has Done*

My father died at home on September 8, 2014, after a long, hard-fought battle with oral cancer. His decline throughout his final year took a heavy toll on Mom. After more than sixty years walking side by side, it was hard for her to see him enter his last days. Even worse, his cancer didn't just attack his body. In many ways, it robbed him of his mind, as well. The sickness affected his thinking and emotions. He'd always been the kindest, gentlest man you could imagine; in his final months, though, his illness made him prone to emotional outbursts. Doctors speculated that the cancer that was ravaging his mouth had moved up into his brain. He wasn't gone completely, however.

We could still see him in there, laughing and loving with us behind those twinkling eyes that had watched us grow up. But none of us could deny the fact that the spark was fading. My mother was watching her best friend, partner, and beloved husband die a slow death right before her eyes, and there was nothing she could do about it.

This torment was especially frustrating for my mother because she could never get a moment's peace. Whereas she'd spent a few decades in relative quiet, enjoying her days alone on the farm and her nights with Dad, suddenly her house was buzzing in a nonstop uproar of activity. A hospital bed was brought in for Dad's comfort, and he rarely got to leave the confines of his makeshift home-hospital room. Along with the special bed came an oxygen tank and a roomful of supplies and chatter, all adding to the cacophony of noise that made the once-quiet farmhouse feel more like an ER. Worst of all, though, was the total lack of privacy. Nurses and caregivers attended to my father around the clock. Mom couldn't walk down the hall without tripping over a nurse or hospice worker. All she wanted was a final few months in relative peace with Dad. She got the opposite. As his health and mind faded, she got less and less of him and more and more of the strangers who were brought in to help.

Of course, she appreciated everything they did to extend his life and make him comfortable, but it became a bit much by the end. She was conflicted. A quiet house would mean he was gone, and that thought was hard for her to bear. But she rarely talked about what she'd do when he passed; that was a worry for another day. As long as her Truett was still with her, she was going to do what she'd always done: laugh, love, and pray at his side. She didn't want to waste a single minute worrying about when he'd leave her; she just focused on making the most of whatever time they had left.

Finally, on Friday, September 5, 2014, the nurses called the family together and told us that Dad only had a day or two left. Nearly our entire family filled the house that weekend. We spent most of Friday and all of Saturday together in Dad's bedroom talking, sharing stories, singing hymns, and sometimes sitting in silence as we each tried to say goodbye to him in our own way. Some of the grandchildren were in and out of the house all weekend while others slept on sofas. On Sunday, though, the crowd began to break up as the grandchildren had to return home for work or school. By Sunday night, September 7, it was down to Dan, Bubba, John, and me. And, of course, my mother. She sat by Dad's bed holding his hand that entire weekend.

Around 10:00 p.m., Mom—in her early nineties—had to get some rest. It had been such a long, emotional day. The nurses told her it would still be a few hours before Dad would likely pass, so Mom decided to go to bed for a little while.

Before she left the room, though, Mom gave Dan and Bubba strict orders: "Do not let me sleep through this, boys. When it's time, promise me that you'll come get me. I simply cannot let him go without me being right there with him. Do you understand me?" My brothers agreed, assuring her that they'd come get her as soon as it was clear he was in his final moments. With that promise, Mom gave Dad a kiss and started off for bed.

Before laying down, Mom took the same handful of pills she took every night at bedtime. That would be a mistake she'd regret for the rest of her life. She was operating strictly on routine at that point and never even considered that her normal evening medicines included a sleeping pill. Once she laid down, the sleeping pill (not to mention the months of mental, physical, and emotional exhaustion) hit her like a freight train. She was out like a light.

A few hours later, around 1:00 a.m., the hospice workers told Dan and Bubba that Dad was almost ready to go. I had gone home to get a few hours of sleep once Mom was tucked in, but I just lived right next door on the farm property. They called me while Dan went into Mom's room to wake her up. He said, "Mom? Mom? Come on, Mom. It's time. He's about ready to go." Nothing. She was in a deep sleep. Dan poked her a bit until she finally woke up a little. She sat up in bed, and Dan said, "Mom? It's time. Come on." She looked at him in a sleepy daze and fell back to her pillow. She simply could not overcome the pull of the sleeping pill she'd accidentally taken just a few hours earlier.

Dan looked at her sleeping so peacefully, unsure of what to do. Finally, when it was clear she couldn't wake up enough to join them in Dad's bedroom, Dan walked out and closed her bedroom door behind him. He wasn't sure if she'd ever be able to forgive him, but he had no choice. As we've all looked back on that night, my brothers and I agree that this was the Lord protecting my mother from seeing and hearing my father's last breath. He passed relatively peacefully, but that is a moment unlike any other. If you've been in the room as someone died, you know exactly what I'm talking about. When the spirit leaves the body, there is a visible change. As Bubba said later, "He choked out his last breath, and then he was gone. Almost immediately, he looked different. His spirit had left, and the shell he left behind was barely recognizable." While his body stayed in the bed, his spirit was soaring. Those in the room with him, though, could only see what was left behind. We could only trust God for the glory we couldn't see with our eyes.

Our family mourned for the next few hours as Mom slept. When she woke up, Dan had to tell her that Dad had already passed. "Oh, Dan!" she cried. "I told you! I told you I wanted to be there with him. You said you'd wake me up. You promised!" All Dan could do was hold her as she wept and pounded her fist. Her Truett was gone, and she had missed it.

That day was a flurry of activity. Dan actually went into the office for a few hours that morning. The Chick-fil-A staff at the Support Center held a weekly Monday morning devotion, and he wanted to take advantage of that time to personally tell the team that Dad had passed. His message was broadcast to the entire Chick-fil-A family through a live stream, giving everyone the chance to hear the news straight from him. Mom, sitting in her robe and pajamas, watched the announcement at her dining room table with Bubba and me on each side.

We never left the house that day, but there was so much going on around us. The nurses had begun to break down Dad's makeshift hospital room and their cramped nursing station in his bedroom. The phone rang a lot. Bubba and I tried to shield Mom from as much of the commotion as possible, but the whole day was exhausting for all of us. At some point that afternoon, Mom turned to me and said, "Since your Dad's gone, does that mean there won't be any nurses coming in and out of the house anymore?"

"No, Mom," I replied. "Everyone's gone. You don't have to worry about them anymore. The house is yours again." She breathed a huge sigh of relief and a little smile crept across her lips. It was the first smile I'd seen all day. Knowing she'd be able to walk around her house without hearing the machines beeping and nurses chatting gave Mom the first true moment of joy she'd had in a while. Even though Dad was gone, Mom still had some life left to live. And, finally, she was free to live it in her peaceful little farmhouse.

A few days later, hundreds of people joined together to celebrate the life and legacy of S. Truett Cathy. Dan, Bubba, and Dan's son Andrew got the chance to speak, honoring the man to whom we owed everything. Others gave eulogies, telling stories about Dad and reminding us all of how funny, quirky, kind, generous, and loving he was. It was a huge celebration, but there was a distinct down-home feel to the whole thing. This wasn't the passing of a simple business leader or successful entrepreneur. No, this was the celebration of a man of God, a husband, a father, philanthropist, a Sunday School teacher, and a fixture in the community. Mom sat there listening intently to every speaker. She laughed a lot. She wiped away a few tears. She sang praise songs. She chatted quietly with her heavenly Father. She said goodbye to the love of her life. And, as the service was dismissed and the pallbearers carried Dad away, she trailed behind them . . . singing.

Maybe she was overcome with a spirit of worship, or maybe it just felt right for her to usher her beloved husband to his grave the way she had first won his heart—through her sweet, angelic voice. Either way, only her pastor, walking close beside her, heard her singing as they walked down the aisle:

> To God be the glory, great things He has done!
> So loved He the world that He gave us His Son,
> Who yielded His life an atonement for sin,
> And opened the life-gate that all may go in.

Praise the Lord! Praise the Lord! Let the earth hear His voice!
Praise the Lord! Praise the Lord! Let the people rejoice!
O come to the Father, through Jesus the Son,
And give Him the glory! Great things He has done!

O perfect redemption, the purchase of blood!
To every believer the promise of God!
The vilest offender who truly believes,
that moment from Jesus a pardon receives.

Praise the Lord! Praise the Lord! Let the earth hear His voice!
Praise the Lord! Praise the Lord! Let the people rejoice!
O come to the Father, through Jesus the Son,
And give Him the glory! Great things He has done!

Great things He has taught us, great things He has done,
And great our rejoicing through Jesus the Son;
But purer and higher and greater will be
Our wonder, our transport, when Jesus we see.

Praise the Lord! Praise the Lord! Let the earth hear His voice!
Praise the Lord! Praise the Lord! Let the people rejoice!
O come to the Father, through Jesus the Son,
And give Him the glory! Great things He has done! [3]

Even on what must have been the saddest day of her life,
Mom lifted her voice in praise to her heavenly Father.

Her marriage, her ministry, her whole life can be summed
up in the last phrase she uttered as she left the sanctuary with my

3   "To God Be the Glory," Words: Fanny Crosby, 1875. Music and Setting: William
    Howard Doane, 1875. Public Domain.

father that last time: "O come to the Father, through Jesus the Son, and give Him the glory . . . great things He has done."

The End of the Beginning

Right after Dad's funeral, my granddaughter Ashlynn walked up to Mom, took her hand, and said, "GG, I'm so sorry. We're all going to miss him so much, but I know it must be so much harder for you."

Mom smiled her sweet smile and said, "Thank you, honey. But it's okay. He's in a much better place, and I'll be there with him soon enough." None of us realized how true that would be.

Jeannette McNeil Cathy followed her husband onto glory only ten months later. Speaking at her funeral, Bubba joked, "Mom always knew Dad hated being alone. I'm sure that's why she followed him there so quickly."

All three of us—Dan, Bubba, and myself—took turns remembering our mother during her celebration of life service. Standing before the large crowd of friends and family, Dan confessed to a lot of trouble he put Mom through. That was fitting, because Bubba also confessed—to even *more* trouble Dan put her through. Even at her homegoing service, her boys were trading barbs and joking around with our ever-patient, ever-playful mother.

Although she survived Dad by only ten months, Mom still did a lot of living in that short time. With the constant pressure of Dad's declining health behind her (and with the hundred health-care workers out of her hair), Mom seemed to enjoy the opportunity to "get back to [her] life." She carried on her unending conversation with her heavenly Father, of course. The talks were louder and longer now that she didn't have to worry about a houseful of nurses and medical techs walking in and out all the time. She also committed herself even further to the study of the Word. If she was at home, we knew we'd find her watching one of her favorite TV pastors deliver a powerful message. She filled page after page (and pantyhose backboard after pantyhose backboard) with sermon notes and deep spiritual insights. Following her doctor's orders, she also jumped back into painting and created some of our family's enduring favorites, such as the portrait of my granddaughter Reese and the unfinished portrait of Dad we found in her studio closet. She had lunches with friends and reconnected with those in her church family that she hadn't seen in a while, and she even tried to teach herself how to use an iPhone so she could stay in touch with everyone more easily. All in all, that final year was a happy time for her—except for the iPhone. She never got the hang of it.

Mom did get lonely in the house at night, however. There were many evenings when she called the farmhand, Chris, after dinner. She'd say, "Chris, I know this could wait until morning, but one of the lightbulbs in my bathroom went out. Could you come over here and change it for me real quick?" Chris knew what she was really asking for: *company*. Fortunately for us, Chris and his wife loved my mother dearly. He'd come replace the lightbulb and end up watching TV with her for an hour or so just to help her pass the time.

Mom's health remained strong during that year. She followed Dr. Wilmer's instructions to the letter, even riding her stationary bike three miles every single day right up until the end. Things had gone so well, in fact, that we were all surprised when she grew ill so quickly in late July 2015. We were all at a family waffle dinner on a Sunday afternoon at Dan's house. That's where Mom met her newest great-grandchild, Maverick Cathy—her twentieth great-grand. We got the picture of Mom holding Maverick that I mentioned earlier, and then, with Maverick still in her arms, she began to feel very uncomfortable. My sister-in-law Cindy could tell something was wrong, so she took the baby from her and called Bubba, who had gone off to Dan's horse barn with some of the other children. Bubba rushed back to the house to take Mom home.

When they got to the farmhouse, Bubba and Cindy got Mom into her pajamas just before sunset. Bubba had his ukulele with him, and he was strumming away in the kitchen as Mom and Cindy walked in from the bedroom. Bubba said, "Mom, come look at this sunset! It's beautiful tonight!" She walked over and they stood there enjoying the magnificent view of the sun setting at the edge of the family farm. Bubba started plucking out Mom's favorite non-church song, "Somewhere Over the Rainbow," and they all began singing along, standing there in the kitchen where we'd spent so much of our lives.

I took her to the doctor the next morning, Monday. The discomfort she had been feeling was fluid collecting around her heart. Dr. Wilmer told her what was happening and said he could perform a somewhat risky procedure to help prolong her life, but there were no guarantees. In her typical fashion, Mom replied, "Charles, I know where I'm going when I die. But, if I can hang around a little longer, and if this surgery will help you by giving you a little more practice, then let's do it. Either way, I'm not that worried about what'll happen to me." They scheduled the surgery for that Thursday, but Mom didn't make it that long. She passed away peacefully surrounded by her family on Wednesday, July 22, 2015.

I could write a dozen more books about my mother and still never even scratch the surface of what all she meant to me, our family, and everyone whose life she touched. She was the very definition of *remarkable* in every sense of the word. She taught me just about everything I know that's worth knowing. And, if her life has any lesson for you, it's the lesson she started this book in the introduction. That lesson is, *you can*.

If Mom were here today, she'd want you to know what she told so many other people throughout her life. *You can*. You can overcome humble, even horrible circumstances. You can have a personal, intimate relationship with a heavenly Father that will never leave you or forsake you. You can do more, go further, and dream bigger than you ever imagined. You can find a love that lasts a lifetime with your perfect soul mate. You can sing and you can dance. You can learn from books, lectures, sermons, radio, and television. You can get an education no one expects you to get at a school no one expects you to attend. You can teach yourself home appliance repair and how to get pony and motorcycle stains off white carpet. You can do real, life-changing ministry with a "chicken man." You can have the richest life of your dreams no matter how much or how little money you have. Whatever your situation, whatever you want to do, wherever you want to go, *you can*. You. Can. More specifically, as Mom always said, "You can . . . *with God!*"

That's just one lesson my mother taught me in our sixty years together. I can't wait to see her again in heaven so she can spend all eternity teaching me many, many more.

Acknowledgements

This book has been a labor of love for me, and it would not have been possible without the encouragement, help, and support of several special people:

My husband, John. The idea for this book came from a conversation he and I had one night. As he and I laughed while sharing stories about my mother, he began to encourage me to write these things down. As we discussed it, we realized that much has been written about my father, but almost nothing has ever been written about Mom. The more I thought about it, the more I believed this could be a wonderful resource for our family, giving future generations the opportunity to truly get to know the incredible lady behind the man. With this book, I pray our family and many others can get to know her and love her—almost as much as we do! So, thank you, John, for your encouragement and prodding in making this book a reality. More importantly, thank you for loving my parents so well.

Allen Harris, whose amazing gift with words helped me turn these sometimes-unbelievable stories into something readers might actually believe.

All the grandchildren and great-grandchildren who made my mother's life so vibrant and rich. She loved every single one of you!

The many family members, friends, and loved ones in our Chick-fil-A family who graciously shared their stories and unique perspectives for this book.

To our heavenly Father, whose faithfulness always put a song in Mom's heart and whose forgiveness through His Son, Jesus Christ, has given all her children, grandchildren, and their spouses a home in heaven someday with Him and with her.

This is our story, this is our song, praising
our Savior all the day long!

Endorsements

"*A Quiet Strength* is the remarkable story of Jeannette M. Cathy. I'm sure you're familiar with her husband, S. Truett Cathy, founder of the legendary Chick-fil-A, but in these pages, you'll read the behind-the-scenes story of this beloved family's matriarch. She lived her life with courage, dedication, and a firm belief that, because of Jesus, 'You can!'"

SHEILA WALSH, AUTHOR OF *PRAYING WOMEN*

"Jeannette Cathy dances, sings, and prays her way across the pages of her daughter's delightful portrait of her. This small woman was by no means 'Fatherless,' and was way more than the 'lady behind the man.' Instead, this spirit was a force to be reckoned with, who catapulted her children and grandchildren into the next generation with holy intension and the power of a dynamo."

GLORIA GAITHER, LYRICIST, AUTHOR, AND SPEAKER

"Jeannette Cathy lived a life so beautiful and so impactful that it makes perfect sense to turn her legacy into a lovely compilation of stories and principles. Having known and loved Jeannette personally, I can tell you this book is not to be missed. You will treasure what you learn from her quiet strength, steadfast commitment to family, and solid walk with God. Chick-fil-A's faith-based ethics and strong business sense have been on display for years, but now we get an insider's view into the life of the Cathy family with Jeannette as matriarch and heartbeat of the home. In writing about her mother, Trudy Cathy White has given us a gift we won't soon forget."

LYSA TERKEURST,
#1 *NEW YORK TIMES* BESTSELLING AUTHOR
AND PRESIDENT OF PROVERBS 31 MINISTRIES

"As the daughter of a strong, determined woman myself, I recognize much about the remarkable life of Jeannette Cathy as told in *A Quiet Strength*. Through all of her family's success, they never lost their servant hearts thanks to her humble leadership. It's not surprising that this successful, faith-centered company had behind it a woman of such strong character."

AMBASSADOR NIKKI HALEY

"What a joy to see a book on the inspiring life of my dear friend, Jeannette Cathy. She was not only the beloved wife of Truett but [she] was also a godly and encouraging influence to all who knew her. Trudy Cathy White, Jeannette's daughter, does a beautiful job recounting her life with delightful anecdotes that depict the Christ-centered values and principles that governed Jeannette's interactions with others. I trust whomever reads this memoir will be blessed."

DR. CHARLES STANLEY, SENIOR PASTOR OF FIRST BAPTIST
ATLANTA AND PRESIDENT OF IN TOUCH MINISTRIES